MYANMAR
in Pictures

Tom Streissguth

Twenty-First Century Books

Contents

Website address: www.lernerbooks.com

Twenty-First Century Books
A division of Lerner Publishing Group, Inc.
241 First Avenue North
Minneapolis, MN 55401 U.S.A.

CULTURAL LIFE 46

► Religion. Art and Architecture. Festivals and Holidays. Literature. Music. Sports. Food.

THE ECONOMY 56

► Agriculture, Fishing, and Forestry. Services and Tourism. Transportation and Communications. Energy, Mining, and Manufacturing. Foreign Trade and the Black Market. The Future.

FOR MORE INFORMATION

Library of Congress Cataloging-in-Publication Data

Streissguth, Thomas, 1958–
    Myanmar in pictures / by Thomas Streissguth.
        p.   cm. — (Visual geography series)
    Includes bibliographical references and index.
    ISBN: 978-0-8225-7146-9 [lib. bdg. : alk. paper]
    1. Burma—Juvenile literature. 2. Burma—Pictorial works—Juvenile literature. I. Title.
DS527.4.S84 2008
959.1—dc22   2006034987

Manufactured in the United States of America
1 2 3 4 5 6 - PA - 13 12 11 10 09 08

INTRODUCTION

The Union of Myanmar, called Burma until 1989, is the largest nation in Southeast Asia. The country has been through a turbulent history, with many conflicts between rival kingdoms and ethnic groups. Burma was a colony of Great Britain before its independence in 1948. In the first years of independence, the country prospered from foreign trade and achieved one of the highest standards of living in the region. But under British rule, the people were unable to develop strong economic or political institutions of their own. Their economy weakened, and the country fell under harsh military rule.

Myanmar's 51 million people benefit from the country's fertile land and abundant natural resources, including timber, oil, and gemstones. Myanmar holds the world's largest forest of teak, a valuable hardwood. The country allows foreign firms to collect natural gas—an important source of income.

But even with these resources, Myanmar has not prospered since the early 1960s, when the nation went through drastic changes. In

1962 a military junta, or committee, took control of the government. The government took ownership of all industry, including farming. Burma isolated itself from the rest of the world and cut business ties with other nations. A corrupt government took most of the income from the country's valuable exports. The junta banned elections and opposing political parties and censored all media. The police and the armed forces harshly controlled the citizens.

Although other nations imposed economic sanctions (penalties), the junta defied demands to allow free elections. In 1990 the junta simply refused to accept the results of an election that would have allowed an opposition party to have power. The junta also paid little heed to environmental damage. Clearing of tropical forests for timber, farmland, and fuel caused many forests to disappear. Although the government banned the export of logs, illegal timber cutting continued in remote areas.

After the junta's founding, Myanmar became one of the world's poorest countries. Once the biggest producer of rice in the world,

Inset map labels

CHINA
JAPAN
Tibet
MYANMAR
(BURMA)
SOUTH
KOREA
INDIA
South
China Sea
PACIFIC
OCEAN
VIETNAM
CAMBODIA
MALAYSIA
SINGAPORE
INDIAN
OCEAN
AUSTRALIA

0   1000 Miles
0   1000 KM

Main map labels

INDIA

Ledo

CHINA

Vochan

BANGLADESH

Chindwin R.

Ayeyarwady R.

Mu-se

Maubin

Monywa

Mandalay

Inwa

Yandaboo

Kyaukse

Bagan

Daunggyi

Inle Lake

LAOS

Mekong R.

Ayeyarwady R.

Naypyidaw ✪

Thanlwin R.

Natmauk

Taungoo

Bay of
Bengal

Sittaung R.

Shwegyin

Pathein R.

Bago

Pantanaw

Yangon R.

Bago
R.

Thaton

THAILAND

Pathein

Martaban

Myon Mya

Yangon
(Rangoon)

Gulf of
Martaban

Mawlamgine

Yadana Gas Field ▪

Yetagun
Gas Field ▪

Ayutthaya ▪

A n d a m a n
S e a

Mergui
Archipelago

Gulf of
Thailand

Legend

Myanmar
(Burma)

⸻ International border
⸻ Ledo Road
✪ Capital city
● City
∴ Ruins

0   150 Miles
0   150 KM

N

Myanmar had to start importing this important crop. In the cities, unemployment rose and living standards fell. Basic medical services, household goods, and even electricity grew scarce. Unable to find work, start a business, or leave the country, millions of families struggled to survive.

Meanwhile, along the country's borders, ethnic minorities took up arms against the government. The fighting killed thousands and drove many people into refugee camps along Myanmar's eastern border with Thailand. To fight the conflicts, the junta spent its scarce resources on the military. The government made little investment in education, public transportation, or economic development. Nor has it been able to halt drug smuggling in the eastern region known as the Golden Triangle (an area shared with Thailand and Laos). In this area, smugglers collect and transport vast amounts of opium, the raw material of the illegal drug heroin.

The shape of Myanmar looks a little like a parrot flying westward. Its upswept wings form the three northern states, its head faces the ocean, and its tail stretches down the peninsula.

In the early twenty-first century, Myanmar has taken some steps to end its isolation. The government encourages tourism. It welcomes new business investment from India and China, two of Myanmar's neighbors. But the economy still struggles, and the government does not allow democratic elections or political openness. The people of Myanmar have experienced more than four decades of dictatorship, or absolute power in the hands of the junta. They face many tough challenges in the years to come.

THE LAND

Myanmar's area of 261,789 square miles (678,034 square kilometers) makes it slightly smaller than Texas. Myanmar borders Bangladesh to the west, India in the northwest, and the People's Republic of China in the north and east. A short border with Laos lies north of the long frontier between Myanmar and Thailand, which runs south into the Malay Peninsula. (A peninsula is land that is nearly surrounded by water.)

The Andaman Sea—a part of the Indian Ocean—touches the southwestern coast of Myanmar. The Gulf of Martaban meets the northern limits of this sea. It lies west of the wide delta (where a river meets the sea) formed by the Ayeyarwady River. To the northwest, the Rakhine seacoast faces the Bay of Bengal. This coast continues north from the Ayeyarwady delta to Myanmar's border with Bangladesh.

◉ Topography

The topography, or landscape, of Myanmar is varied. The country has tall mountain ranges, fertile river plains, and long seacoasts. The

coastline of Myanmar runs for about 1,650 miles (2,655 km). Five main regions make up the geography of Myanmar.

In the Northern Mountains region, along the border with China, rises the Hengduan Shan range. It is part of the Himalaya mountain chain, which crosses southern Asia. The rugged Kachin Hills also lie within this northern region. The highest point in the country is Mount Hkakabo, which rises to 19,295 feet (5,881 meters) at the northern limit of Myanmar.

The Eastern Mountains region of Myanmar includes the Shan Plateau. The elevated flatland of the plateau borders Laos and Thailand. Few roads cross the steep hills and dense forests of this region. Armed forces patrol the Eastern Mountains to battle militias. These small armies have been fighting Myanmar's government for decades. The government has closed much of the area to outsiders. The mountains extend southward into the long, thin Tenasserim Coast, which borders the Andaman Sea.

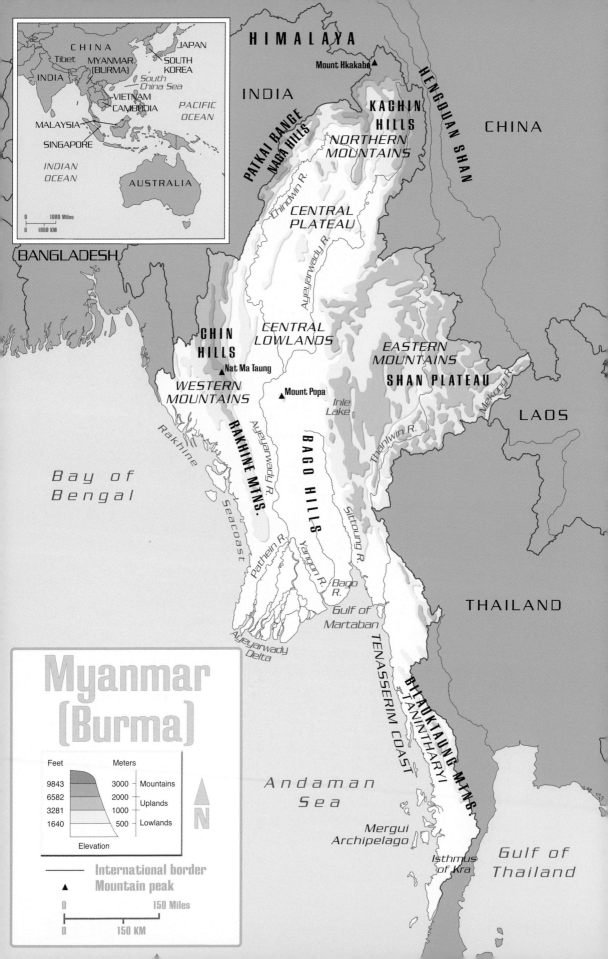

HIMALAYA

Mount Hkakabo ▲

INDIA

KACHIN HILLS

HENGDUAN SHAN

CHINA

PAITKAI RANGE

NAGA HILLS

NORTHERN MOUNTAINS

Chindwin R.

CENTRAL PLATEAU

Ayeyarwady R.

BANGLADESH

CHIN HILLS

CENTRAL LOWLANDS

EASTERN MOUNTAINS

Nat Ma Taung ▲

WESTERN MOUNTAINS

▲ Mount Popa

SHAN PLATEAU

Inle Lake

Mekong R.

LAOS

Rakhine Seacoast

RAKHINE MTS.

Ayeyarwady R.

BAGO HILLS

Thanlwin R.

Bay of Bengal

Pathein R.

Yangon R.

Sittoung R.

Bago R.

Gulf of Martaban

THAILAND

Ayeyarwady Delta

TENASSERIM COAST

BILAUKTAUNG MTNS.

TANINTHARYI

Myanmar (Burma)

Feet	Meters	
9843	3000	Mountains
6582	2000	Uplands
3281	1000	Lowlands
1640	500	
Elevation		

N

Andaman Sea

Mergui Archipelago

Isthmus of Kra

Gulf of Thailand

———— International border
▲ Mountain peak

0   150 Miles

0   150 KM

Inset map:

CHINA

Tibet

JAPAN

MYANMAR (BURMA)

SOUTH KOREA

INDIA

South China Sea

PACIFIC OCEAN

VIETNAM

CAMBODIA

MALAYSIA

SINGAPORE

INDIAN OCEAN

AUSTRALIA

0   1000 Miles
0   1000 KM

To the west of the Eastern Mountains is the Central Lowlands region. These low plains surround the valleys of the Ayeyarwady and Sittoung rivers. The region has the highest population density in Myanmar. It is also the driest region of Southeast Asia. But irrigation (watering systems) has made it a vital farming region. The kingdoms of ancient Burma had their capital cities here. Thousands of Buddhist temples, many of them centuries old, dot the countryside.

West of the Central Lowlands, the Western Mountains region includes the Rakhine range. These steep slopes run north and south along the Rakhine seacoast, on the Bay of Bengal. The western ranges include the Naga, Patkai, and the Chin Hills. Thick forests of tall pines flourish on the slopes, which receive ample rain. The highest point in this region is Nat Ma Taung, a mountain reaching 10,018 feet (3,053 m). The hills run down to a strip of fertile land along the Bay of Bengal seacoast.

The southern Tanintharyi region is about 50 miles (80 km) wide and 500 miles (800 km) long. The Bilauktaung Mountains skirt the border with Thailand. Offshore is the Mergui Archipelago, a group of about eight hundred small islands. Most of these islands are uninhabited, with no people, buildings, or roads.

WHAT'S WITH THE NAME?

At one time, Myanmar was called Burma in English. The British gave this name to their colony. They called all the people Burmese, although many ethnic groups were present. In the Burmese language, the country was Myanma.

In 1989 the military junta changed the country's name in English to Myanmar. They wanted to erase all reminders of the colonial past. The name comes from two Burmese words meaning "swift" and "strong." Rangoon became Yangon, and the Irawaddy River became the Ayeyarwady. The only major town that didn't change its name was Mandalay.

Governments that do not recognize the military junta do not use the name Myanmar. For example, the United States and Britain officially call the country Burma. Also, *Burmese* remains in common use as an adjective. *Burma* is still the correct name for the historic kingdom and the British colony.

🕜 Rivers and Lakes

The rivers of Myanmar rise in the mountains of the north. They flow southward to empty into the Bay of Bengal. In the Central Lowlands run the two main rivers, the Ayeyarwady and the Thanlwin. The Ayeyarwady flows 1,250 miles (2,012 km) from its source in the Himalayas. The river

SEA GYPSIES

The Salon people—or "sea gypsies"—live among the eight hundred islands of the Mergui Archipelago. They trawl the surrounding waters for fish. Some also engage in smuggling between Myanmar and Thailand. Skilled boatbuilders and deep-sea divers, the Salon live for part of the year on their watercraft. They spend the rainy seasons onshore.

waters fertile plains before ending in a delta. There it branches into nine main streams. This low-lying region holds most of Myanmar's population. Many market towns and Mandalay, the second-largest city of Myanmar, lie on the banks of this river.

The largest tributary, or branch, of the Ayeyarwady is the Chindwin. It joins the river about 70 miles (110 km) south of the city of Mandalay. The Thanlwin River is the most important waterway of eastern Myanmar. It flows for 1,749 miles (2,816 km). The Thanlwin rises in the Himalayas of southwestern China. As it passes through the Shan Plateau, it cuts a series of gorges, or steep, narrow passages. The river's fast current makes it difficult for boats to travel. It empties into the Gulf of Martaban at the port of Mawlamyine. The Sittoung River flows south from the Bago Hills into the Andaman Sea. Only small boats can navigate the rapid currents of this river.

Myanmar's largest lake is Inle Lake, in the southern Shan Plateau. Small villages and monasteries, where monks live, surround the lake. The local Intha people build floating vegetable gardens on the water. Thick mats of water plants along the shallow shores are strong enough to support small homes made of reeds and resting on stilts.

Climate

Myanmar's climate varies with region and elevation, or height above sea level. The north is a temperate zone—marked with variable seasons. The temperatures fall sharply at night. In the tropical south, near the equator, Myanmar experiences higher heat and humidity year-round. The moist air feels heavy and sticky.

Most rain falls between May and October, during the southwest monsoons. These winds blow from

the ocean across Southeast Asia. The winds carry moisture, which they release as rain. In the rainy season, heavy downpours flood the rivers and cause landslides in the mountains. Average temperatures during this season vary from 70°F (21°C) in the Shan Plateau to 80°F (27°C) in the central plains and in Yangon, the capital.

The cool northeast monsoon season runs from October to mid-February. Rains are lighter, temperatures are lower, and the cloud cover is not so heavy as during the southwest monsoons. The average temperature varies between 70°F and 82°F (21°C and 28°C), with Yangon averaging 77°F (25°C) in January. In some of the highlands of the Shan Plateau and in the north, temperatures sometimes drop below freezing.

At the end of this cool season, temperatures rise. They often reach 100°F (38°C) in the lowlands and the delta. April and May are the hottest months of the year. In central Myanmar, temperatures can climb to 113°F (45°C).

Yearly rainfall reaches 200 inches (500 centimeters) along the coast. Rainfall is only 35 inches (89 cm) in the Central Lowlands, where the Rakhine range blocks monsoon rains.

Flora and Fauna

Myanmar has two important zones of vegetation. The monsoon forest, with both dry and rainy seasons, lies north of Yangon. The rain forests, which receive rain throughout the year, cover mountains and coastal areas to the south. Myanmar has the largest surviving rain forest in Southeast Asia, where many forests have been cut down. The monsoon forest trees are deciduous—their leaves drop every year. The rain forests' broad-leaved trees are evergreen.

Myanmar has more than twenty-five thousand varieties of wildflowers, hundreds of different fruit trees, and large forests of bamboo, cane, and rattan. Orchids and other epiphytes perch in forest trees. The roots of epiphytes draw water from the moist air. Thick vines climb up forest trees to reach the light. In the highlands grow a wide variety of tropical hardwoods,

Stilt houses line the shores of **Inle Lake.** Most villagers make money by fishing or growing vegetables on the marshy banks.

Myanmar is home to a small population of rare **Javan rhinos.** In the jungles, roots grow down from the branches of **banyan trees.**

including teak and mahogany. Mangroves flourish in brackish (salty) water. These trees, with their partly aboveground roots, protect the coastlines from high tides and destructive waves. Above the high-tide line grow hibiscus, coconut palm, and casuarina trees.

Due to logging, forests are rapidly dwindling. Though the loss of trees threatens bird habitats, Myanmar still hosts the most diverse bird population in Southeast Asia. Parrots and peacocks add color with their bright feathers. Mountain forests are home to thrushes, lapwings, shrikes, hornbills, and flycatchers. Herons, storks, cormorants, and many other species of waterfowl favor the delta region.

The forests are home to hundreds of mammal species. Scientists discovered the rare and tiny leaf deer in the 1990s. This deer reaches just 20 inches (50 cm) high at the shoulder. Fruit bats feed on fruit trees. These large bats are also called flying foxes. Myanmar has many large mammals, including Himalayan bears, wild pigs, banteng (wild ox), and wild pigs. Big cats include leopards and tigers. The tapir is a hoofed animal with a stubby trunk. Its black-and-white coloring provides camouflage in the shadowy forest. Near the border with Thailand live two rare species of rhinoceros. The

People in Myanmar who follow the Buddhist faith honor the banyan tree—a fig tree that sends out roots from its branches to the ground. The Buddha, the founder of Buddhism, meditated under a banyan until he reached a state of spiritual awakening called enlightenment.

Javan rhino has a single horn, while the Sumatran rhino has two. Myanmar also has the world's largest population of wild elephants. More than five thousand elephants work in construction, farming, and logging.

Four species of sea turtle inhabit coastal areas. Myanmar is also home to fifty-two kinds of poisonous snakes, including cobras, kraits, and vipers. Pythons kill their prey by constricting, or squeezing, them. Growing up to 30 feet (9 m) long, some kinds of pythons can swallow wild pigs whole.

DEATH BY SNAKEBITE

Myanmar has the world's highest rate of death by snakebite. Poisonous snakes include cobras, vipers, and kraits. Kraits are especially dangerous. Krait venom kills by quickly paralyzing victims' muscles, including the muscles needed for breathing. It is sixteen times more deadly than cobra venom. The government closes some foot trails during the nesting season of cobras and other poisonous snakes.

Natural Resources and Environmental Issues

Myanmar holds the largest deposits of oil and natural gas in Southeast Asia. Most of these deposits lie in the Ayeyarwady River valley. Myanmar also mines tin, silver, zinc, copper, gold, lead, coal, marble, and more. Myanmar is famous for its rubies and other precious stones. Miners collect high-quality jade from the northern mountains.

Myanmar's most valuable natural resource is the fertile soil of the central valley and the southern river delta. At one time, this land produced about half of the world's rice. The forests provide valuable hardwoods. Cut teak and mahogany are shipped through the port of Yangon.

Loggers at an elephant camp near Taungoo use **elephants** to move harvested logs. Elephants move through the trees more easily than machinery and cause less damage to the land and vegetation.

A PRECIOUS BELL

The Mingun Bell rings over the historic site of Mingun Paya, a Buddhist temple. The bell is 16 feet 3 inches (5 m) in diameter and weighs 90 tons (82 metric tons). The bell is the largest noncracked, ringing bell in the world. King Bodawpaya, who reigned from 1782 until 1819, ordered the bell to be made. To achieve a smooth and serene tone, metalsmiths cast the bell in bronze, gold, silver, iron, and lead.

Timber cutters, however, damage Myanmar's forests. Farmers cut trees for housing material and fuel. Commercial firms harvest valuable tropical trees. The country loses about 1.5 percent of its forest every year. The rate of deforestation—loss of woodlands—is increasing. When large sections of forests are cut, the trees are often not replaced. This deforestation causes a loss of habitat. As forests disappear, wildlife dies or retreats into more remote regions of the country. The government officially protects more than one-third of its forests. Illegal logging, however, continues in many of these areas. Thirty-seven kinds of plants are threatened with extinction, or dying out.

Loss of habitat and poaching, or illegal hunting, threatens large wild mammals, such as big cats and elephants. Poachers also hunt valuable pythons and forest turtles for their skins and shells. The rhinoceros species of Myanmar have nearly disappeared. Many people believe that rhinoceros horns have medicinal properties, and artists carve them. Ninety-four animal species are threatened or endangered.

Factory waste and sewage runoff pollute many of Myanmar's rivers and its seacoast. This pollution destroys fish and bird species in coastal areas and wetlands. In the delta region, a growing fishing industry has greatly reduced fish populations.

◉ Cities

Though only 29 percent of the population lives in cities, Myanmar's urban population is growing steadily. Many people have moved to cities from rural areas. This has led to overcrowding, unemployment, and pollution in cities.

Myanmar's cities show centuries of different cultural and economic influences. In the city of Yangon, modern offices and hotels surround the **Shwedagon Pagoda,** a complex of hundreds of temples and stupas (shrines) built over 2,500 years.

YANGON (population 4 million) is Myanmar's largest city and its functional capital. (Since 2005 the government has moved many of its offices to Naypyidaw.) Yangon sprawls along the lower Yangon and Bago rivers, on the eastern edge of Myanmar's delta region.

King Alaungpaya founded this city in the 1750s. Hoping for a peaceful reign, the king dubbed the new city Yangon, or "running out of enemies." The city thrived as a seaport and trading center. It became the capital of Burma in 1885, when the British overthrew the Burmese monarchy (royal family) at Mandalay. The British name Rangoon replaced Yangon until the government changed the name back in 1989.

Modern Yangon is a noisy, crowded, and bustling city. Teahouses, small shops, and concrete block apartment buildings line the streets. Scooters, buses, bicycles, taxis, and trishaws (three-wheeled bicycle taxis) jostle with food vendors and pedestrians. Office buildings and small shopping malls cover the southern limits of the city. To the north rise the golden dome and spire of the Shwedagon Pagoda (temple). This important Buddhist structure is visible from anywhere in the city.

Street vendors sell produce and hot snacks beside a busy road in Mandalay. The city's modern office buildings house many of Myanmar's major transportation, export, and communications businesses.

Yangon has common urban problems. These include water and air pollution and a high rate of unemployment and poverty. The government has forced many homeless people to move out of the city center and into northern suburbs. In these areas, health and living standards are low.

MANDALAY (population 2.5 million) is the country's second-largest city. It is in the dry central plains, along the Ayeyarwady River. Mandalay was once an artistic and cultural center of Burma. Artisans, weavers, and writers enlivened the city. It also served as an important trading hub between Southeast Asia and China.

King Mindon Min made Mandalay the capital of the Burmese kingdom in 1857. The British captured the city in 1885. They replaced the monarchy with a colonial government headquartered in Yangon. Fighting during World War II (1939–1945) destroyed much of Mandalay. The royal palace of the fallen Konbaung dynasty (ruling family) also burned to the ground. After the war, the Burmese government rebuilt the palace. Guarded by 26-foot (8-m) walls and a moat of water 230 feet (70 m) wide, it remains an important landmark in the center of modern Mandalay.

After the war, builders also replaced the city's wooden houses and shops with concrete block buildings. Large shantytowns, where living conditions are poor, still surround the city. In the central districts, modern apartments and office buildings rise.

Mandalay is home to many new Chinese immigrants. They control a busy trade in manufactured and agricultural goods with their former homeland. Chinese firms run important service businesses such as banks, insurance, and real estate. The city also has large communities of Nepalese, Indians, and ethnic Shan originally from the highlands of eastern Myanmar.

MAWLAMYINE (population 300,000) lies along the Thanlwin River. It is about 12 miles (20 km) from the Andaman Sea. Mawlamyine served as the capital of British Burma from 1827 until 1852, when it was known as Moulmein. A center of the teak trade, Mawlamyine has a busy river port. About 75 percent of its people are ethnic Mon, with the rest being Burmese, Chinese, Kachin, and Indian.

PATHEIN (population 300,000) lies in the delta region, on the eastern bank of the Pathein River. Pathein has a large river port. It links towns throughout the delta and central Myanmar to the sea. Cargo ships transport Pathein's milled rice and products made at local workshops. Pathein artisans make ceramics and brightly colored parasols known as the Pathein Hti. These lightweight umbrellas are in demand throughout Myanmar.

NAYPYIDAW (population 100,000), formerly Pyinmana, is gradually becoming the junta's seat of government. In 2005 Myanmar's leaders began moving thousands of government workers out of the capital to Naypyidaw. This isolated city in central Myanmar lies about 200 miles (323 km) north of Yangon. The junta renamed this city Naypyidaw, meaning "royal city." By moving into northern Myanmar, the government has a stronger presence near regions where antigovernment rebels are operating. Myanmar's ruling generals also want to isolate themselves from any future unrest in Yangon.

Visit www.vgsbooks.com for links to websites with additional information about the history and people of Myanmar's cities. Discover the cultural and political influences, such as ethnic minorities and religious traditions, that give each city a unique character.

HISTORY AND GOVERNMENT

Archaeologists believe that Stone Age people inhabited the valley of the Ayeyarwady River almost five thousand years ago. The earliest known settlers were the Mon people, who arrived in Burma from central Asia. The Mon settled in the lower Thanlwin and Sittoung river valleys. According to Mon chronicles, their first kingdom, Suwarnabhumi, began in 302 B.C. The capital of this state was at Thaton.

The Mon traded throughout southern Asia by land and sea. They exchanged goods with Cambodia, India, and towns around the Mekong River delta of Vietnam. They adopted Buddhism. This belief system began in fifth-century B.C. India. The Mon were the first people in Burma to practice Buddhism.

In the first century A.D., the Pyu migrated into Upper Burma (the northern half of the country). They came from Tibet and the remote valleys of the Himalaya mountains. They prospered by trading with both China and India. In addition, people from China's Yunnan Province, northeast of Burma, arrived in the central river valleys. They

eventually moved into Siam (present-day Thailand). Their descendants, the Shan, settled in eastern Burma.

Bamars, Mon, and Kublai Khan

The central plain of Burma was the scene of conflict between the Bamars (or Burmans) and the Pyu. The Bamars had come from present-day Gansu Province in China. Eventually, they emerged dominant in central Burma. They cultivated rice and took control of the main trading routes to China and India. In the ninth century, they established a walled capital at Bagan (also spelled Pagan) on the Ayeyarwady River. This ancient city lies near Mandalay.

Anawrahta became the king of the Bamars in 1044. An ambitious ruler, Anawrahta intended to bring all the scattered towns of Burma under his authority. In 1057 Anawrahta demanded the Tripitaka, Buddhist holy books, from King Manuha of the Mon. These were the oldest and most authoritative source on the teachings of the Buddha.

Their possession brought the owner honor and authority over Buddhists. Manuha refused to give up the books. Anawrahta then besieged and captured Thaton. He made thousands of Mon officials, as well as the king and his family, his prisoners at Bagan. The scriptures were carried back to Bagan on the backs of thirty-two white elephants, considered sacred animals. Anawrahta unified Burma under a single ruler for the first time.

> **The great Bamar king Anawrahta was a capable ruler and an unbeaten warrior. But his death came during peacetime. A rampaging water buffalo killed him in the year 1077.**

In 1077, after Anawrahta's death, his son Sawlu became king. He reigned until 1084, when the Mon killed him during a revolt. The next Bamar king, Kyanzittha, managed to put down the Mon rebellion. He kept the Bamar empire stable and prosperous. Kyanzittha arranged the marriage of his daughter to a prince of the Mon royal family. Their son, Alaungsithu, became Kyanzittha's heir.

Meanwhile, the capture of the Tripitaka from the Mon gradually changed the culture of the Bamars. They adopted a written Mon language. They also took up the Theravada system of Buddhism from the people they had conquered.

The Bamar kingdom became a powerful state. A network of irrigation canals and dikes allowed Bamar farmers to grow rice on a large scale. The Bamar raised hundreds of elaborate temples at Bagan. But Buddhist monks, who controlled land as well as trade, represented a rival power center to the royal dynasty. The Shan also remained independent of the Bamar kings.

In the thirteenth century, the Mongol ruler Kublai Khan came to power in China. The Yuan dynasty he began conquered much of eastern Asia. But the Bamar king Narathihapate (reigned 1254–1287) defied Kublai Khan's demand for tribute, or payments. In 1277 the king led an army into China to battle the Mongols. Afterward, his own son poisoned him. The Bamar army challenged the Mongols again at the Battle of Vochan in 1287. The battle ended in a Bamar defeat.

Kublai Khan

After the Battle of Vochan, the Bamars submitted to the Mongols. But foreign rule of Burma was brief. The Yuan dynasty of China collapsed in the late fourteenth century. The Bamar army crushed a revolt by the Mon. The Bamars then built a new capital at the northern city of Inwa.

The Bamar realm entered a golden age. Its cities flourished, and Bamar artisans created elaborate temples. The writers of the royal court produced the classical works of Burmese literature. But the Mongol conquest had weakened Bamar authority. The Shan and the Rakhine peoples defied the Bamar kings. The Mon rebuilt their dynasty at the town of Bago. They fought with the Shan for control of Lower (southern) Burma.

Bamar Kingdoms

Nicolo di Conti, from the trading city of Venice, Italy, visited Bagan in 1435. Later in the fifteenth century, the Portuguese set up a trading post in Goa, India. From this post, Portuguese ships sailed to the cities of the Burma coast, trading for teak and gemstones. The Portuguese also sent trading missions to the cities of Siam.

In 1519 the Portuguese merchant Anthony Correa made a trade agreement with the viceroy (ruler) of Martaban, a port on the Andaman Sea. The Bamar king Tabinshwehti opposed the treaty. But the king was also having trouble with rivals in the mountains of Burma. These groups had remained independent of the Bamar kings. The Shan had already founded an independent capital and invaded the central plains. Burma became a scene of chaos and conflict. The fighting destroyed many towns and holy sites. The Shan overran the Bamar capital in 1527.

In 1531 the Bamar king moved to the city of Taungoo. From this new capital, King Tabinshwehti reunified Burma. He attacked the viceroy of Martaban in 1541. This led to the first conflict between Europeans and the people of Burma. Portuguese soldiers defended the port of Martaban. But Tabinshwehti hired more Portuguese soldiers to fight for him. They helped him conquer the city and drive the Portuguese from Martaban.

Tabinshwehti then returned the capital to Bagan. His brother-in-law Bayinnaung (reigned 1551–1581) conquered Ayutthaya, the capital of neighboring Siam. These successful campaigns drained the kingdom's treasury, however. The weakened Bamar state became vulnerable to outsiders arriving from Europe.

In 1600 Philip de Brito of Portugal arrived in Rakhine. De Brito was of humble origins, and he was ambitious. He brought a large company of soldiers from Goa, India, and built fortifications in Rakhine. He then conquered Bagan and ruled the Bamars for thirteen years. In 1613 the Bamar king Anaukpetlun defeated the Portuguese. He captured and executed de Brito by impaling him on a stake. Anaukpetlun then reunited the Bamar kingdom.

Thalun, the successor to Anaukpetlun, moved his capital to Inwa, the former capital in the north. Thalun spent more on religious observances and temple building than on defense of his state. In addition, Inwa's location in the north made it difficult for the Bamars to defend their seacoasts and trade. European raiders and navies sailed freely in the coastal waters. They staged raids on Bamar ports and shipping. They also stirred up rebellion among the king's subjects.

The British Conquest

Other European states were sending trading missions to southern Asia. The British, Dutch, and French built small trading posts. These nations dealt in gemstones and in Burma's abundant rice crop. They also meddled in the country's politics. The French encouraged a rebellion by the Mon against the capital of Inwa. In 1752 Inwa fell to a Mon army.

Afterward, a commoner named Alaungpaya rallied a Bamar army. Alaungpaya fought the Mon as well as the foreigners. The Bamars captured Inwa and Bagan. Alaungpaya then built a new capital at Yangon. The long and bloody campaign drove the Mon into eastern Burma and Siam. In 1760 Alaungpaya died. His son and successor, Hsinbyushin, conquered the Siamese capital at Ayutthaya.

Meanwhile, the British Empire was expanding in southern Asia, seeking to control its natural resources. The British established a colony in India in the middle of the eighteenth century. In 1819 the British invaded Burma. They conquered Rakhine and several other cities. The First Anglo-Burmese War (1824–1826) ended in a British victory and the Treaty of

British troops move artillery into Burmese territory during the **First Anglo-Burmese War.**

Yandaboo. The British sought a secure land route from India to Singapore, a British post at the southern tip of the Malay Peninsula. To achieve this, the British provoked the Second Anglo-Burmese War in 1852. The British conquered the province of Bagan and Yangon. They extended their control to what they called Lower Burma.

Angered by the foreign presence, the Burmese revolted against their king, Pagin Min. His half brother Mindon Min (reigned 1853–1878) replaced him. Mindon Min established a new capital at Mandalay. Far from the seacoast, which the British controlled, Mandalay could more easily resist British rule. Intending to modernize his realm, the king sent representatives to western Europe on fact-finding missions. He nationalized the new oil industry and built the country's first small factories.

The British accused Mindon Min's successor, Thibaw Min, of siding with the French, who were also seeking colonies in Southeast Asia. Using this excuse, Britain declared war on Burma again. The Third Anglo-Burmese War, in 1885, resulted in the British claiming the entire country. They made it a province of their empire of India. The colony's capital was at Rangoon. This conflict ended the Burmese monarchy.

Resisting the British

As a British colony, Burma became an important center of rice cultivation. The colony also provided teak, oil, and gemstones. The British brought in large groups of laborers, many from India. These workers cleared tracts of land for rice growing. Foreigners controlled trade in the country's valuable resources. Burma's farmers and city dwellers did not benefit. In the cities, Burmese workers competed against Indian immigrants for scarce jobs. Unemployment among the Burmese ran high.

Britain set out to modernize its colony. The British ordered the building of roads, railways, schools, and hospitals. Paved roads and electricity went into the large cities. A few Burmese from important families went to Great Britain for higher education.

The University of Rangoon, the first university in Burma, opened in 1920. This university soon became the center of resistance to British rule. Violent student demonstrations took place during the 1920s. An anti-British group known as the Thakin (masters) formed. The British had required university students to address them with this term. The Thakin protested British rule in articles and pamphlets.

The growing unrest persuaded the British to allow a Burmese legislature in 1923. This lawmaking body had very limited powers. But it did provide the Burmese an opportunity to organize their struggle against colonial rule.

In 1930 Saya San, a Burmese doctor, led a revolt in the countryside north of Yangon. Saya San proclaimed himself the king of Burma. Thousands of peasants and laborers joined his movement. But the better-armed British forces crushed the rebellion in 1932.

The revolts and strikes forced the British to make some changes. Burmese leaders wrote a new constitution in 1935. The constitution kept a British governor. It also created a nine-member cabinet to advise the government. The legislature helped to choose the cabinet members. Nevertheless, the next year, a general strike took place. Burmese workers and students stayed home to protest British rule of the colony.

On April 1, 1937, the British separated Burma from India. A new constitution set up an elected assembly. Ba Maw, leader of the Sinyetha (Poor Man's) Party, became the first prime minister. He served until 1939. The British arrested him in 1940 for plotting against British rule. The politician U Saw became the new prime minister. ("U" is a title, similar to "Mr.")

The Thakin, led by Aung San, emerged as a strong rival party. Aung San had organized a group of anti-British rebels known as the Thirty Comrades. The group trained in Japan to resist the British.

Meanwhile, Japan was building an empire in Asia. In 1941, as part of its plans for expansion, Japan joined with Germany to fight

The people of Burma often attached the names of spirits or animals to groups of people. The followers of Saya San called themselves *galons* after a mythical bird. During World War II, the *chindits* were rebel bands that fought against Japanese control of Burma. The chindits were named after ferocious lions known as the *chinthes*. These animals guarded palaces and temples when Burma was an independent monarchy.

against the British Empire and its allies during World War II. At the height of its powers, Japan invaded Burma in 1942. That year, the Thirty Comrades returned to Burma. They fought alongside the Japanese army against the British.

The invasion forced the British to retreat to India. The Japanese army occupied Yangon, the capital. They released Ba Maw from prison and appointed him prime minister. Aung San then became the leader of what would become the Burmese National Army. Although Japan promised independence, the Japanese army did not give up control over Burma's cities or resources. This angered Aung San, who secretly organized resistance to Japan.

During 1944 British, U.S., and Burmese forces steadily pushed the Japanese out of northern and central Burma. U.S. troops built the Ledo Road across northern Burma. The road linked India and China. It allowed the Allies to supply food and weapons to anti-Japanese forces in China. Road builders faced bad weather, landslides, thick forests, and the deadly disease malaria.

In March 1945, Aung San led an open revolt against the Japanese. The Japanese abandoned Burma in May. In August Japan surrendered, and World War II came to an end.

During World War II, the Japanese disrupted the supply of oil to British ships. Here Japanese soldiers attack the **Yenangyoung oil fields** near Mandalay.

AN OIL STRATEGY

At the beginning of the twentieth century, oil became a valuable commodity. In the United States and Great Britain, naval ships began to burn oil rather than coal. These new ships demanded a constant supply of fuel. Great Britain had to import its oil from other countries, such as its colony of Burma. In the 1920s, several U.S. companies asked permission to explore Burma for oil. But the British refused. They kept Burma's reserves for British ships alone. These vital oil supplies were the main reason Britain held on to its colony until after World War II.

GENERAL STILWELL ADVISES HIS TROOPS

U.S. general Joseph Stilwell gave the following instructions to U.S. soldiers going to Burma during World War II.

- **NEVER fool with a water buffalo. That animal is bad medicine and has no respect for the American uniform.**
- **Soldiers are not expected to go around maltreating large trees, but some of the Burmans venerate these objects and so a special warning is required on the point. Treat every Burmese tree as respectfully as if it were a California Sequoia or Redwood.**
- **Take off those issue shoes before entering any Burmese pagoda or other holy place. The Burmans require it. It's like taking off your hat before entering an American church.**
- **Burma is overrun with dogs. The Burmans don't take good care of them but they are resentful if anyone else mistreats them. The barking of the dogs may disturb your sleep at night. Don't throw a shoe; you will need it.**

from "A Pocket Guide to Burma," online at http://cbi-theater-2 .home.comcast.net/booklet/ guide-to-burma.html

⊙ Independence

After World War II, a British governor returned to control Burma. Burma remained a British colony. The British promised independence to the Bamars. However, ethnic minorities would remain under the rule of a British administration. Aung San grew unhappy with the delay in independence. He organized strikes and protests against British policy. Finally, Aung San made an agreement with the British in January 1947. The agreement set up an assembly to write a new constitution. The British promised full independence the following year.

The Anti-Fascist People's Freedom League (AFPFL) emerged as the dominant pro-independence political party in Burma. Some members of the AFPFL opposed the agreement made with the British. The former prime minister, U Saw, was also angered by being left out of the new government. In July 1947, U Saw arranged the successful assassination of Aung San and several cabinet ministers.

On January 4, 1948, the Union of Burma achieved independence from British rule. The constitution created a bicameral (two-house) legislature. Burma developed quickly in the early years of independence. Infrastructure (public works) built by the British helped land and sea transportation. A brisk export trade allowed the economy to grow.

While the standard of living improved, the government still fought uprisings among ethnic minorities along the border. The Shan and others sought their own independent regions. In addition, a civil war in China began affecting Burma. A Communist army was fighting for control of China. (Communism is a political system in which the government controls the economy, in theory to ensure economic equality.) Chinese troops crossed over the border. They seized control of mountainous regions in north and east Burma.

In these areas, farmers began growing opium poppies. These flowers provide the raw material for the drug heroin. Money from the illegal trade helped to pay for anti-Communist rebellion in southern China. It also paid for arms bought by the Shan, who were fighting the Burmese government in the northeast.

Military Takeover

President U Nu became the first prime minister of independent Burma. He ordered the government to seize private companies created when Burma was a colony. This policy did little to help Burma's economy develop, however. The new state companies were corrupt and inefficient. Burma's exports fell steadily through the 1950s. In 1962 U Nu prepared to privatize (return state companies to private ownership).

Burma's leading army officers opposed the plan. Many of them ran the state companies themselves. U Nu's plan threatened their authority and their wealth. In 1962 General Ne Win led a military coup to overthrow the government. Ne Win established the Revolutionary Council of army officers to govern Burma.

All farmland was government-owned by 1965. Farmers had to pay rent for their land. The junta set low, fixed prices for the rice crop. Without incentives, farmers didn't maintain their fields. Rice farming demands constant maintenance of watering systems and land. Rice production fell. Eventually, the country had to import rice.

The council suspended the constitution and closed down the legislature. The council also canceled Burma's scheduled elections. Ne Win ordered the arrest of U Nu and several other leading politicians. The general became the prime minister and the head of the new Burma Socialist Programme Party, or BSPP.

Shortly after the coup, Ne Win ended privatization. He announced a new program called the Burmese Way to Socialism. In a Socialist state, the government strictly controls the economy. Manufacturing and mining companies again came under state control. The state cut off trade with most foreign countries. Burma imposed strict censorship on books and media. The authorities jailed opponents of the regime or forced them to leave the country.

In 1974 Ne Win closed down the Revolutionary Council. He created a new People's Assembly. The assembly had no independence from the military junta. The economy of Burma continued to struggle. Prices steadily rose higher. Without foreign trade, the country did not attract new investment. The state faced a heavy load of debts to foreign nations and banks.

Fortune-tellers are very popular in Myanmar. General Ne Win often relied on their advice. It is said that he once changed the direction of traffic within twenty-four hours because of such advice. Many traffic accidents resulted.

The Coup of 1988

Opposition to the junta increased in the 1980s. Students led strikes in the cities, challenging the junta's control. The army also faced rebellion in the ethnic states. Burma was spending most of its scarce resources on the military. Its army, known as the Tatmadaw, became the strongest in Southeast Asia. Without funds to repair infrastructure, the country's roads crumbled. In some years, the entire education system shut down. The people of Burma also faced severe shortages of rice, a staple food.

On August 8, 1988—a date chosen for its lucky run of 8s—civilians confronted police during a march in Yangon. Police and troops opened fire on demonstrators, killing hundreds. Meanwhile, Aung San Suu Kyi, the daughter of Aung San, had returned to Burma from her home in Britain. She was a charismatic speaker and leader. She rallied opposition to the government.

The demand for democratic government grew more violent. On September 18, another army coup ended the BSPP's control of the government. Army officers established the State Law and Order Restoration Council (SLORC). General Saw Maung headed this junta.

The SLORC imposed a strict curfew in Yangon. The junta banned all gatherings of more than five people. Anyone speaking or writing against the regime risked arrest.

To head off further protest, the SLORC announced elections. The government allowed a new political party, the National League for Democracy (NLD), to form. Aung San Suu Kyi became the head of this party. But the junta arrested her in July 1989 for speaking out against the junta. That same year, the junta changed the English name of the country from Burma to Myanmar.

Myanmar held legislative elections in May 1990. The NLD won 392 of the 485 seats in the legislature. Ethnic minority parties won another 65. The SLORC did not accept the election results. The junta arrested many of the winners from the NLD. Others fled to form a government in exile, the National Coalition Government of the Union of Burma. Eventually, the members of this government set up their headquarters in the United States.

The SLORC imposed harsh rule over Myanmar. Its generals wanted to eliminate all opposition. The junta forced people out of the cities to the countryside. They made them to work without pay on roads and other construction proj ects. Many foreign governments

Aung San Suu Kyi stands with a portrait of her father, Aung San.

AUNG SAN SUU KYI

Aung San Suu Kyi is the daughter of Aung San, a leader of Burmese independence. Her mother, the ambassador to India, brought her to India when Aung San Suu Kyi was fifteen. There she studied the life of Mohandas Gandhi, the Indian leader who preached nonviolent protest.

Suu Kyi returned to Myanmar in 1988 to help her dying mother. The same year, violence against Myanmar's regime broke out. Suu Kyi founded the National League for Democracy. In 1990 her party won elections. But the government denied the victory and refused to allow Suu Kyi to become prime minister. Instead, the junta made her a prisoner in her own house. Aung San Suu Kyi became widely popular within Myanmar and abroad. But she was not willing to lead a violent revolution against the government. She called for nonviolent protest. For this stance, she won the Nobel Peace Prize in 1991.

condemned these measures. The United States and other countries ended diplomatic relations with Myanmar.

In April 1992, General Than Shwe replaced Saw Maung as head of the SLORC. General Ne Win remained the true leader of Myanmar. The junta took steps to respond to protests, both at home and abroad. It released Aung San Suu Kyi from house arrest in 1995. The same year, the junta staged a national convention. It invited the NLD to help write a new constitution. This document, however, would leave Myanmar in the hands of a military regime. The NLD withdrew from the convention. The SLORC renamed itself the State Peace and Development Council (SPDC) in 1997.

Myanmar in the Twenty-First Century

Aung San Suu Kyi continued to speak out against the junta and visit supporters. The junta again put her under house arrest in 2001. To protest Myanmar's regime, many foreign nations have imposed embargoes, banning private companies from trading with or investing in Myanmar. General Ne Win died in 2002, but the government's rule remained the same.

In 2003, to protest Suu Kyi's house arrest, the United States banned trade. The ban does not include aid to combat poverty and hunger. The ban has hurt Myanmar's garment industry, which exported clothing to the United States. As a result, many textile workers have lost their jobs. To cope with the loss of income, Myanmar's regime has invested in the tourism industry. The country allows visitors, with few restrictions on where they can travel. Income from tourism helps to keep the struggling economy afloat.

Myanmar's security forces number almost half a million members of either the military or the police, in a nation of only 51 million people. The government spends almost 10 percent of the national income on the army and police, who closely watch the population.

In addition, armed groups are still fighting in eastern Myanmar. Ethnic minorities such as the Shan want to govern themselves independently of the regime. Guerrillas move from place to place. These small groups of rebels stage hit-and-run attacks on public buildings, army posts, and power lines. The army conducts sweeps throughout the various ethnic regions. They question civilians they believe support the opposition groups. Thousands of people have left their land to avoid the

Boys drill in one of Myanmar's guerrilla armies. **Child soldiers** fight with Myanmar's army and in the rebel groups that oppose it. Some children volunteer to fight because they are homeless or starving, while others are kidnapped by soldiers and forced to fight.

conflict. Refugees fleeing to neighboring Thailand live a bare existence in crowded and unhealthy refugee camps.

Early in the twenty-first century, the government reached a cease-fire agreement with most of the ethnic factions. In addition, the junta released several thousand political prisoners. It also tried several army officers for corruption. This did not end opposition to the regime. In Yangon opponents set off several bombs in 2005. A government-in-exile still presses for free elections.

The government continues to ignore these demands. It also continues to censor media and to arrest opponents. Trade embargoes remain in effect. Complex government rules regarding land ownership continue to hamper rice farming. In spring 2006, the government extended Aung San Suu Kyi's house arrest for another year. In early 2007, the government-run newspaper accused her of spending her Nobel Prize money outside Myanmar in order to avoid paying taxes. The new accusations will make it even more difficult for her to campaign for freedom in her country.

Government

Myanmar passed its present constitution on January 3, 1974. The SLORC suspended this constitution after the coup of September 1988. The government announced a national convention to draft a new constitution in 1993. This body suspended itself in 1996. It met again in 2004. The SLORC did not allow the NLD opposition party to participate. No new constitution has been agreed upon. According to the 1974 constitution, citizens over eighteen are eligible to vote, but no elections are being held.

The SLORC became the State Peace and Development Council in 1997. This committee of nineteen includes the heads of the Tatmadaw, or armed forces, and district commanders. The chairperson of the SPDC is also the head of state. A prime minister serves as the head of government. The SPDC appoints the members of the cabinet, some of whom are civilians rather than members of the military.

The legislature of Myanmar consists of a unicameral (one-house) People's Assembly. The 485 members of this body are supposed to serve four-year terms. But the assembly has not been allowed to meet since the last elections of 1990.

Workers build a new road in front of the government's headquarters in the new capital city of **Naypyidaw.** The junta celebrated the official opening of the city on March 27, 2007. However, many of the roads, shops, and schools needed for workers and their families were still under construction.

Visit www.vgsbooks.com for links to websites with additional information about political developments in Myanmar. Learn about the latest news from the new capital city, Naypyidaw, and the efforts to stop violent clashes between guerrilla fighters and the army.

The constitution of 1974 established a new judicial system. The Council of People's Justice functioned as the nation's supreme court. But the coup of 1988 shut down this system. The military junta appointed five judges to a new Supreme Court. In effect, this system operates at the command of the SPDC, the military committee that governs Myanmar. State, division, town, and village courts decide local cases.

Myanmar includes fourteen administrative units, including seven states and seven divisions. The states were formed after independence in 1948. They are meant to allow Myanmar's ethnic minorities some control over their homelands. The Rakhine State, for example, is home to the Arakan (or Rakhine) people. At the local level, people's councils govern towns and villages.

THE PEOPLE

Myanmar's last official census in 1983 counted a population of 35,306,189. Current estimates place the country's population at about 51 million. This number is growing at the rate of 1.1 percent every year. At this rate, about 59 million people will live in Myanmar by 2025.

The population density of Myanmar is 195 people per square mile (75 people per sq. km). In Southeast Asia, population density averages 326 per square mile (126 per sq. km). Myanmar is less crowded than Cambodia but more so than Laos. In addition, Myanmar's population is largely rural. About 71 percent of its people live in the countryside, in farming villages. The highest population density is near the Ayeyarwady River. The government has exiled many of its opponents from the cities to remote towns in the countryside.

Ethnic Groups

Myanmar is home to several different ethnic groups. The largest group is the Bamar. They make up about 67 percent of the population. The Bamar

dominate the central valleys and plains. They also form a majority in the delta region of the south. Before Myanmar was a colony, the Bamars ruled the country from their capitals of Bagan and Mandalay. In modern times, they still hold most of Myanmar's political and economic power.

The remaining ethnic groups have mostly settled in the mountainous regions of eastern, western, and northern Myanmar. They have some control over their own states. They have their own flags, distinct languages, and governing councils. But the military government represses their culture. For instance, the government does not allow teaching in languages other than Burmese, the official language. Those who don't follow Buddhism also experience discrimination.

The Shan, the largest ethnic minority, comprise about 9 percent of the population. They live in Shan State and the surrounding Shan Plateau region. Shan people also live in China, Laos, and Thailand. The Shan practice both Buddhism as well as animism, a traditional belief in natural spirits. Their language is similar to Thai.

Merchants and customers drift through the floating market in the village of **Ywama.** The village is located on the edge of Inle Lake in Shan State.

In the late twentieth century, the Shan carried out the largest uprising ever against Myanmar's government. Shan leaders have called for complete independence for Shan State as well. The government of Myanmar has responded by raiding Shan villages. Many refugees have fled across the border to Thailand.

The Karen, or Kayin, make up about 6 percent of the population. They live south of the Shan in Kayah and Kayin states. Their ancestry is Thai and Chinese. Many of them practice Christianity. The Karen National Union is a large guerrilla group operating in Kayin State. The Karen never signed a cease-fire agreement with the government—one of the few groups that hasn't.

The Kayah, or Karenni, live in an isolated region of eastern Myanmar. They make up about 4 percent of Myanmar's population and mostly earn a living by farming. Their traditional red garments have led them to be nicknamed Red Karen.

The Kachins, comprising about 2 percent of Myanmar's people, inhabit the remote Kachin State in northern Myanmar. They are mostly rice and sugarcane farmers. They also work in forestry and mining, and some make a living in the trade of goods, sometimes illegally, across the border to China.

Chins live in Chin State, near Myanmar's frontiers with India and Bangladesh. The Chin make up about 2 percent of the population. They are hill tribes that live by farming, hunting, and some logging. Many Chin migrate seasonally in search of factory work in Myanmar's cities or seasonal farmwork such as the harvest of sugarcane in the central plains. Some Chin women wear distinctive facial tattoos. Most of the Chin practice Christianity.

The Rakhine comprise about 4 percent of the population. Most live in coastal areas of Rakhine State, near the border of Bangladesh. Although they are mostly Buddhist, a minority practice Islam, the dominant religion in Bangladesh. The Rakhine who are Muslim, or followers of Islam, call themselves Rohingya.

The Mon people were the rulers of Myanmar before the Bamars. They introduced writing and Buddhism to Burma. But the Bamars overcame Mon rule in the eighteenth century. Since then the Mon have passed down many traditions to the Bamars, the majority ethnic group. Traditional Mon culture and language survive in rural areas of the southeast. Altogether, the Mon comprise 3 percent of Myanmar's people.

Women of the Kayan people are known for their neck rings. Their subgroup is also called Padaung, a name meaning "long neck" in Burmese.

AN OLD CUSTOM

The Padaung people of Kayah State practice an old custom of fitting brass rings around the necks of young girls. The first ring is fitted at the age of five or six. Every two years, a new ring is added. The rings weigh down the collarbone. This gives the impression that the neck is growing longer. In this way, some Padaung women have their necks stretched as much as 10 inches (25 cm) by the rings. They cannot remove the rings, as this would cause their neck muscles to collapse. According to Padaung lore, the rings were originally meant for protection against attacks by tigers.

IT'S *NOT* A SKIRT

The *longyi* is a traditional article of clothing for Burmese men and women. Also called a sarong, it is a piece of cotton or silk wrapped around the waist and falling to the shins or ankles. By tradition, men knot theirs in front. Women tuck their longyis in at the side of their waist. The longyi comes in all colors and patterns. Men favor darker colors and checks. Women wear lighter colors and flower patterns. The longyi helps the wearer to stay cool in Myanmar's fierce heat and humidity.

Myanmar is also home to small groups of foreign merchants and workers. These include Bangladeshi, Indian, and Chinese. Together they make up about 3 percent of the population. Since the 1980s, large numbers of Chinese immigrants have sought jobs and business opportunities in Mandalay and northern Myanmar. Many of them come from China's Yunnan Province. They bring distinctive food and customs from that region.

◉ Languages

Burmese, one of the Tibeto-Bamar languages, is the official language of Myanmar. About four out of five people in Myanmar speak it as their first language. Like many other

The *longyi* is a versatile garment worn by men and women. It can be tied in different ways, depending on the wearer's preferences. These women have tied their *longyi* slightly higher to make it easier to walk.

Asian tongues, Burmese is a tonal language. That is, its words change their meanings depending on the speaker's use of a rising, falling, or steady tone.

Many dialects, or variations, of Burmese exist. The standard and official dialect in Myanmar is that of Yangon. A formal version of the language is used in media, in official pronouncements, in speeches, and on ceremonial occasions. People converse in a colloquial (everyday) form of Burmese.

Ethnic minorities in Myanmar speak more than one hundred languages. The most common are Shan, Kachin, Karen, Mon, and Chin. The Shan speak a Thai-related language. The Mon of Lower Burma and the Palaung of the east speak a Mon-Khmer language. Recent immigrants from China speak Cantonese and Mandarin. In the west, some new arrivals use Hindi, Urdu, or Tamil—all languages from India. Others speak Bangla (Bengali), the official language of Bangladesh.

Many Burmese in contact with foreigners speak English. In Asia often two people who do not share a language use English. Instruction in this language begins in primary school. Many students take English classes throughout their schooling.

Pali is a scholarly language. The authors of sacred Buddhist texts used it in their works. Monks in Myanmar have a basic understanding of Pali. Some Pali words have found their way into Burmese. Sacred

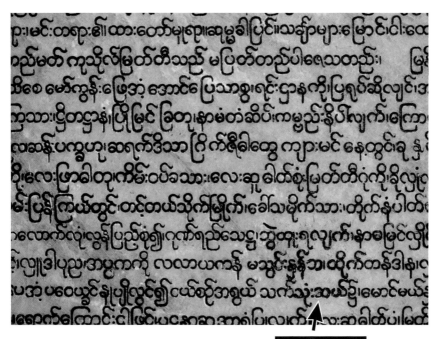

The Burmese language is written in Burmese or **Myanmar script.** The letters are round because they were traditionally written on palm leaves, which can tear when the pen makes a straight line.

chanting within monasteries also takes place in Pali.

Health

Myanmar faces many difficult health issues. The country has few large hospitals or clinics. Many smaller towns and villages have no doctors. A shortage exists of modern medical equipment. Diseases such as malaria affect many of the rural and mountainous areas. Myanmar has high rates of typhoid fever, tetanus, and the lung disease tuberculosis. A worsening problem is dengue fever. Like malaria, dengue fever is carried by mosquitoes. The government of Myanmar has announced the building of new clinics. Vaccination programs are in place to immunize against disease. Still, the government spends less than 1 percent of the national income on health services.

Poor sanitation, especially in urban areas, brings frequent disease outbreaks. Water quality is low in some villages. Shallow wells and small freshwater holding tanks supply water in the countryside. This method allows mosquitoes to breed and spread waterborne diseases, such as cholera and dysentery. Rural villages and some urban neighborhoods also have high rates of malnutrition, due to poor diet.

The infant mortality rate (IMR, the number of babies who die before their first birthday) is an indicator of a country's overall health standards. Myanmar's IMR stands at 75 deaths per 1,000 live births. This is high for Southeast Asia, which averages 34 per 1,000. But Myanmar's rate is lower than the rates of Cambodia or Laos. Life expectancy in Myanmar averages 60 years—57 for males and 63 for females. In Southeast Asia as a whole, life expectancy has reached 69 years.

The guerrilla conflict in the border areas has affected public health. The fighting has cut off hundreds of villages from basic services. These regions have few health facilities. Communication with other regions and large cities is poor. If a disease outbreak occurs, help is slow to arrive and conditions worsen.

Natural disasters also cause public health crises. Myanmar is subject to heavy monsoon rains, river flooding, mountain landslides, and occasional earthquakes. In late 2004, a devastating tsunami hit the coastal areas of Myanmar. This tidal wave washed away several dozen small villages. Rushing water destroyed crops and fields. Seawater and

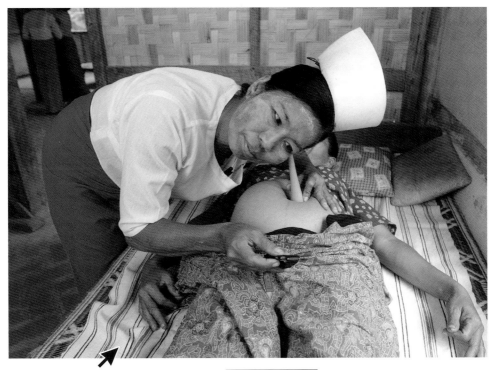

Daw Tin Kyi, a midwife in a village in the **Magwe division,** uses an ear cone to listen for a fetal heartbeat. Rural health centers like hers use both traditional and modern medical equipment to assist women who live in remote areas.

pollutants contaminated local water wells. With the help of some international organizations, such as the Red Cross, many hard-hit areas were able to care for the sick and injured and to rebuild homes.

Myanmar is also struggling with a high rate of HIV, a virus associated with acquired immunodeficiency syndrome (AIDS). Myanmar recorded its first case of AIDS in 1991. Since then the rate of infection has risen to 1.3 percent. A lack of information about prevention has contributed to the high rate. Southeast Asia as a whole has an average HIV infection rate of 0.5 percent. Myanmar has taken some limited steps to combat AIDS through education. Nevertheless, the disease is spreading from high-risk groups—sex workers (prostitutes) and drug users who share needles—into the general population.

Visit www.vgsbooks.com for links to websites with detailed information about public health issues in Myanmar. Read about the national health organizations and international aid organizations that seek to solve the country's unique health problems.

SUNBLOCK STYLE

For a natural sunblock and as makeup, Burmese women and children use a paste made from the bark of the thanaka tree. They apply thanaka paste to the cheeks and forehead. People who work all day in the sun apply it to their entire face, like a mask. City dwellers need less protection, but they may use the paste to paint stylish patterns on their cheeks.

⊙ Women

By law and custom, women in Myanmar enjoy equality with men. Education at all levels is open to both sexes. Families encourage their daughters to attend school. Women can enter almost any profession they choose. Their salaries are equivalent to those of men with the same positions. Women also can own property, and wives and husbands share goods equally in marriage. A married woman keeps her own name. In many instances, she keeps track of the household's money and spending.

Many women in Myanmar are business owners. On city streets, they sell food, jewelry, and small household goods. Some lend money, a profession that serves the needy who cannot borrow funds from a bank.

Some professions are still closed to women in Myanmar. The country's military and government are all male. Buddhist religious teachers and leaders also exclude women from their ranks. In addition, women and men both suffer persecution if they publicly disagree with the government. In rural areas, women and men are subject to work that is forced on them by the government.

⊙ Education

Education in Myanmar begins at the age of five. All students are required to attend elementary schools, which run for five years. Students take an exam to move up to secondary school. These are open to students for another five years. Less than half of all eligible students, however, attend secondary schools.

In addition, Buddhist monasteries and other religious institutions offer education to elementary-age children. These schools teach basic reading, writing, and math, as well as the teachings of Buddhism. The

Many boys are educated at **Buddhist monasteries.** As novices, or young monks, they learn to read and write, and they study Buddhism. Most do not stay at the monasteries, but some choose to become monks as adults.

number of private schools is growing. Most of them offer English-language instruction.

The government encourages English learning as well. In the universities, English has become the main language of instruction. The government links English-speaking with modernization and better ties with the outside world.

Universities at Yangon and Mandalay and four additional colleges provide higher education. But Myanmar's universities and training schools lack basic equipment and facilities. In addition, a shortage of trained teachers exists at all levels. Many of those seeking advanced degrees move to Thailand or Singapore for their studies.

Since the early twentieth century, the universities have been central to political opposition. After the coup of 1988, the junta closed the universities. They remained closed through most of the 1990s. To cope with student protests, the government moved the university in Yangon to an isolated neighborhood. In addition, the police and government closely watch all teaching and student gatherings for signs of political activity.

Myanmar has a high rate of literacy—about 90 percent of the population is able to read and write. This rate is similar to that of Southeast Asia as a whole. The government runs literacy programs for adults and children who can't attend school. People value reading material of all kinds. Many people spend their free time reading novels, nonfiction books, magazines, and newspapers.

CULTURAL LIFE

The people of Myanmar take pride in their country's history and culture. The time as a British colony did not change this outlook. They held strongly to their traditional dress and their religion. Modern Myanmar is strengthening ties to the Western world and allowing more outside visitors. But its arts, literature, and family customs remain distinctly Burmese.

◐ Religion

About 90 percent of Myanmar's people practice Buddhism. Missionaries, who arrived to teach religion, and traders from India first brought this belief system to Burma in the third century B.C. The Mon people of southern Burma practiced Theravada Buddhism, the most common form in modern Myanmar. Theravada Buddhism is also the main faith of neighboring Laos, Thailand, and Cambodia. The other major branch of Buddhism, Mahayana, is more common in China. Ethnic Chinese who live in Myanmar follow this faith.

Buddhists follow the teachings of Siddhartha Gautama, an Indian noble who lived about 2,500 years ago. As Buddha (the Enlightened One), he taught self-awareness and meditation. In the Buddhist view, every living thing experiences birth, death, and rebirth. To escape this endless cycle, an individual must practice right living. This means no lying, stealing, killing, drinking, or improper sexual behavior. It also means charity toward Buddhist monks and to Myanmar's many temples. This brings merit and good fortune to the individual.

Monks wearing bright orange or red robes are a common sight in Myanmar. Every young Buddhist boy attends a monastery for a period of time. Monks seek alms (charity), hold religious ceremonies, and study. Women can become nuns, although it is not as common as men becoming monks. The monks live in monasteries. Most monasteries have cells (small simple rooms) for the monks and a small temple. Visitors come to worship and pay their respects.

Myanmar also has a small non-Buddhist population. Many people of Indian ancestry, about 4 percent of the population, follow Hindu teachings. The Christian faith arrived with foreign missionaries in the nineteenth century. Muslims, who make up another 4 percent, follow the teachings of the Arab prophet Muhammad. Many Muslims live in Rakhine State, near Bangladesh.

The government allows freedom of religion. But the government has also discriminated against non-Buddhists. In some places, they cannot meet to worship or openly practice their faith.

About 2 percent of the people are animists. They worship spirits found in the natural world. The animist view survives in remote hill regions, home to Myanmar's ethnic minorities.

Many of those who practice traditional Buddhism also believe in a family of *nats,* or spirits. The nats do both good and mischief. They live in natural places, such as springs and mountaintops. They can also be present near large trees, cross-roads, or buildings. They visit

GOLD LEAF

Devout Buddhists make regular visits to shrines, where they show reverence to the image of Buddha by bowing, praying, and applying gold leaf to statues. Several workshops in Mandalay specialize in the making of gold leaf. Workers pound paperlike sheets of gold with wooden mallets for several hours, then place the leaves between sheets of oiled paper. The leaves are tissue thin and extremely light. They must be handled with great care. Over the years, some popular statues have gained thousands of layers, which can make the features of the Buddha's face hard to see.

ceremonies, festivals, or performances of music and dance. There are thirty-seven important nats. Small shrines to please the nats are present in many homes and outdoors. The shrines are miniature wooden temples placed on prominent places or on a pole. Garlands of flowers, dishes of fruit, and other offerings adorn the shrine.

Thagyamin is the most powerful nat of all. Every April, according to tradition, he arrives to record the individual's good or bad deeds. Many Burmese also believe in a personal guardian spirit. This spirit attends to the person's needs and oversees conduct and speech.

◉ Art and Architecture

The traditional art and architecture of Burma reflects Buddhist themes and beliefs. Religious art survives throughout the country. It decorates the *payas* (shrines and temples) built in holy places associated with the Buddha or attached to a monastery.

The *zedi* is a Buddhist shrine, usually built of brick. It houses one of the Buddha's relics, or sacred remains (hair, teeth, or footprints).

Although wooden zedi were common in the past, these structures did not survive the centuries of weather and conflict. The traditional zedi has a bell-shaped roof, often covered in gold leaf, ending in a tall spire. Monks meditate and converse on the plazas surrounding these structures, and visitors come at all times to make offerings of food, money, or goods.

King Anawrahta established the ancient capital of

A gilded Buddha reclines in the **Hpo Win Daung Caves** near the city of Monywa. Devoted artists filled the caves with paintings and statues in the seventeenth and eighteenth centuries.

Bagan in the eleventh century. A millennium later, Bagan is the largest archaeological site in Southeast Asia. The many palaces and homes of this city, all built of wood or bamboo, have disappeared. More than twenty thousand religious shrines and temples of every size and description survive. Artists covered the interior walls of these temples with colorful fresco paintings, made by applying paint to fresh plaster walls. Many temples in Bagan have not yet been restored or fully excavated.

The most famous modern Burmese artist is Bagyi Aung Soe (1923–1990). This painter made a thorough study of Burmese history and culture. He attempted to depict Buddhist teachings directly in his works. He suffered poverty and isolation in his time, however, and never found success within his country.

In the past, Burmese sculpture decorated temples and palaces. The Mahamuni Buddha is Myanmar's most famous sculpture. It stands 13 feet (4 m) high. Sculptors created this bronze figure in Rakhine State in the eighteenth century. King Bodawpaya then brought it to a shrine in Mandalay, where it remains.

Traditional sculptural forms include sculptures of the Buddha and the nats in wood, bronze, alabaster, or ivory. Other art forms include silk embroidery and clothing, stone carving, and jewelry making. Burmese artisans are also famous for marionettes, made from painted and glazed clay. Puppeteers control these jointed figures' movements with dozens of strings.

Festivals and Holidays

A festival of lights takes place in Myanmar each October, at the time when rivers run high. On Inle Lake, people place images of the Buddha aboard ceremonial barges. The statues shine with gold. The barge rowers bring the golden Buddha statues from one monastery to the next.

In Myanmar the calendar includes several religious festivals, known as *pwe*. These can last for several days, and everyone takes part. During a pwe, an entire town or village turns out to enjoy music, dancing, and games. Local monks hold ceremonies at monasteries and pagodas and lead processions through the streets.

The most important pwe, Thingyan, is a nationwide water festival. It lasts several days in April, the traditional new year. Monks wash statues of the Buddha. Children and students offer gifts to their parents and teachers. Participants relieve the heat and humidity of the season by

This altar celebrates the **nats of Mount Popa,** a volcano believed to house some of the most powerful spirits. Many pilgrims visit Mount Popa during two yearly festivals, one in spring and one in fall.

flinging water balloons at passersby. They spray one and all with water from hoses and jars. Water throwers spare only pregnant women, the police, and monks and nuns. According to belief, the water cleanses the troubles of the past year.

The festival of Buddha takes place in May. This was the time of the Buddha's birth, his attainment of nirvana (enlightenment), and his death. Beginning with the full moon in July, devout Buddhists observe a period of spiritual preparation. They give up all worldly pleasures and study the scriptures and teaching of the Buddha. Buddhists believe this is an unlucky time for moving, courting, or weddings.

December is the time of the nats and their festivals. In January temple festivals take place throughout the country. An annual rural festival, Htamane, takes place in February. Farmers offer sticky rice with sesame, peanuts, ginger, and coconut in thanks for a good harvest.

National holidays include Independence Day on January 4. This holiday celebrates the end of British rule. March 27 is Armed Forces Day. May 1 is the traditional Workers' Day. July 19, Martyrs' Day, marks the assassination of Aung San in 1947.

TEA TIME

Tea shops are an important part of daily life for many city dwellers in Myanmar. Many people spend hours at the local tea shop. They read, watch the street life, meet friends, and talk. But if they talk about politics, they are careful not to be overheard and reported to the government. Waiters prepare pots of tea in many varieties, served to each customer's taste. They also set out clear, hot tea in flasks. Tea drinkers add milk, honey, or sugar to their tea.

◉ Literature

Burmese writing has a long and rich history. The oldest known texts are verse plays and poetry celebrating the life and teachings of the Buddha. Court poets entertained the king and his followers with stories from the Ramayana. This epic of heroes and spirits came from India. Prose works recount the history of Burma and the teachings of Buddhism. *The Burmese Chronicle*, the longest such work, dates from the early eighteenth century. It is still a popular book in modern Myanmar.

In 1904 James Hla Kyaw (1866–1920) adapted stories from *The Count of Monte Cristo*, a novel by the French writer Alexandre Dumas, into Burmese. This work became the foundation for modern fiction in Burma.

Writers created the Khitsan or the "New Writing" movement in the early twentieth century. Their books contain fictional stories, poetry, and Buddhist sermons. Thakin Kodaw Hmaing (1876–1964), a journalist, poet, and playwright, wrote novels about Burmese history and the drive for independence from British rule. The political themes of his books inspired nationalism and great cultural pride among Burmese readers.

In the years before World War II, literacy and printing grew more widespread. Literary journals met a rising demand for new writing. P. Monin and Shwei Udaung were the leading writers of the mid-twentieth century. U Maung Gyi (1878–1939), a former Buddhist monk, wrote historical novels about the kings of Burma.

U Nu (1907–1995), a prime minister of Burma, wrote *Thaka Ala*. This well-known play criticizes corrupt politicians, both those in power and those in opposition. Two of his plays—*It's Just Cruel* and *The Sound of the People Victorious*—explore strong political themes. The latter was made into a comic book as well as a movie during the 1950s.

Dagon Taya (b. 1920), a leading writer of the post–World War II era, created novels, short stories, and poems. He was close to the independence hero Aung San and also outspoken on politics. This landed him in jail for four years after the coup of 1962. Journalgyaw Ma Ma Lei (1917–1982) wrote *Not Out of Hate,* a book about the impact of foreign culture on Burma. *Blood* is her novel about the Japanese occupation of Burma during World War II.

Mya Than Tint (1929–1998) was a skilled translator who worked on many different forms of writing, including novels, short stories, and essays. He was honored for his work with a national prize four times. The Burmese are avid readers of foreign books, when they can find them. This makes translators important and honored individuals in the literary field.

Music

The classical music of Burma accompanies dance performances, plays, or religious ceremonies. Its basic instrument is a small brass gong. A long set of gongs rests in front of the musician. Accompanying the gongs are ensembles of xylophones, flutes, drums, and the *saung,* a small harp. Larger ensembles include bells, *linkwin* (large brass cymbals), and clappers.

Classical music uses variations in tone and rhythm for variety. Clappers and hand cymbals mark the beat. Burmese composers used a system of seven modes (scales) for voice and instrumental melodies. In the past, musicians played traditional music from memory.

Modern popular music takes inspiration from Western styles. Classical styles also often make their way into pop music. In the cities of Myanmar, rock and rap music are popular. But the government bans any political commentary or criticism in song lyrics. Iron Cross, the biggest rock band in Myanmar, formed in 1990. This group has recorded dozens of albums and has toured throughout Asia. Its lead singer, Lay Phyu, appears on posters all over the country.

◉ Sports

One of the most popular sports in Myanmar is kickboxing. This contest tests skill, strength, and stamina. Kickboxers train with masters from a young age in special halls or rural camps. The competitors use their hands, feet, elbows, and knees—but never their heads—in striking their opponents. They combine their attacks and countermoves in dozens of ways.

Kickboxing matches take place during festivals and ceremonies. The music of drums, cymbals, and bamboo clappers accompanies the matches. The national championship takes place every year at Aung San Stadium in Yangon.

Children and adults take part in the national sport of Myanmar, *chinglone* (similar to Hacky Sack). In this game, players form a circle and try to keep a small ball made of rattan or cane in the air. They can use only their legs and feet. On city streets and in squares, chinglone circles are a common sight. The best groups can keep the ball in the air for long periods of time. In competitive chinglone, each team has six players. In one version, they relay the ball over a tall net, as in volleyball.

Soccer, known as football, is a popular street game in Myanmar. A small number of people enjoy golf or tennis. More common pastimes are kite flying and distance running.

THE NUT THAT STAINS

Many people in Myanmar chew betel nut. This bitter nut comes from the tropical betel tree. Betel-nut vendors work street corners. They wrap the nut in leaves. Chewing the bitter betel nut stimulates the nervous system. It's like drinking a strong cup of coffee. The nut also causes reddish brown teeth. People spit out the betel juice as they chew. The telltale traces of betel-nut use are dark stains on the streets and sidewalks.

◉ Food

The food of Myanmar borrows traditional recipes, flavors, and spices from China, India, and Thailand. Big meals start with a bowl of dal, or lentil soup, often with onions, turnips, or potatoes. Main courses often feature a plate of rice with curried chicken or fish. (Beef is taboo to most Buddhists in Myanmar.) Curry dishes blend spices and flavorings such as coriander, turmeric, garlic, ginger, cumin, and lemongrass. *Ngapi*, a sour-smelling fish paste, also flavors many dishes in Myanmar.

A popular dish in Myanmar is a salad of vegetables and fruit with peanut sauce, pepper, chilies, and lime juice. *Lapet* is a traditional mixture of fermented tea leaves, peanuts, fried beans, and ginger. Cooks add eggplant, beans, corn, potatoes, onions, and squash to many curries, stews, and soups. The fruit selection includes mangoes, pineapple, watermelon, lychees, coconuts, papayas, and bananas. Durian is a tropical fruit with a delicious flavor but a disgusting odor.

People commonly begin their day with *mohinga*. This dish includes rice noodles with chicken or fish—catfish, eels, carp, or even frogs. Cooks add sliced onions, chilies, and wedges of lemon or lime. Shan noodles are stir-fried with thinly sliced pork and vegetables. Burmese kitchens also prepare chicken and fish soups and omelets of egg and sausage. Beef and fish salads are popular. The Burmese also sample a variety of fried insects, including crickets, grasshoppers, and beetles.

Desserts include baked puddings, often made from coconut milk. Other favorites include cakes, ice cream, fried bananas, and jaggery—the sweet and boiled juice from a palmyra palm tree. Sugarcane juice, teas, bottled water and soda, and coffee are the major drinks. Alcohol is less common, as traditional Buddhist teachings forbid it.

SPICY SWEET POTATO IN COCONUT MILK

Coconut milk, extracted from coconut meat, is a popular ingredient in many Burmese dishes. To reduce the fat content, buy low-fat coconut milk. Be careful handling the chili pepper—its juice can burn skin and eyes. Grate the gingerroot with a cheese grater.

1 c. canned coconut milk

1 c. water

1 tbsp. lemon juice

1 chili pepper, such as jalapeño, seeded and finely chopped

1 inch fresh gingerroot, grated

1 onion, chopped

2 garlic cloves, crushed

1 tsp. ground turmeric

½ tsp. salt

⅛ tsp. black pepper

1 lb. sweet potatoes, peeled and sliced

1. Place all the ingredients except the sweet potatoes in a large saucepan. Bring to a boil, stirring occasionally. Then turn the heat to low, and simmer for 5 minutes.
2. Add the sweet potatoes to pan. Mix well, and bring back to a boil. Turn heat to low, cover pot, and simmer for 20 minutes, or until the potatoes are tender. Test with a fork. Serve hot.

Serves 4

THE ECONOMY

Myanmar has many valuable natural resources such as oil, gemstones, and timber. The country also benefits from fertile and productive land. Under British rule, private companies mined or harvested and sold Burmese goods. These firms used a network of roads, bridges, railroads, and ports to get their products to market. The country also was one of the world's biggest rice growers. Small manufacturing industries employed many people in the cities.

General Ne Win's coup of 1962 damaged the economy. The military junta seized industries and farms and cut off trade with other nations. In search of self-sufficiency, Myanmar lost nearly all of its foreign investment. Government spending and high foreign debt emptied its treasury.

In the twenty-first century, the government still controls oil production, gem mining, forestry, and banking. Military officers control the few private companies. They run these firms for their personal benefit. Companies must pay bribes to government.

In modern Myanmar, unemployment runs high. Without foreign

investment, industries cannot grow. Most farmers struggle to survive on the low prices they get for their harvests. People have little faith in the government's economic policies. They hide their savings rather than deposit it in banks or invest it.

In the past, Myanmar received foreign assistance. Much of this aid stopped in protest of the junta's dictatorship. The United States and other trading partners stopped trading with Burma. Their embargoes shut down many workshops and factories. The country's weak currency and banking system discourage foreign companies from new investment.

In the early twenty-first century, high energy prices, including a rising oil price, helped Myanmar earn more in trade. The gross domestic product (GDP), the total value of the country's goods and services, is about $1,600 per person. This is the lowest GDP in Southeast Asia, which averages $4,530 per person.

Most people in Myanmar do not see the benefits of economic growth. They also must deal with inflation and rising prices. The rising price of fuel, for example, causes hardship for those who rely on vehicles to make a living. In addition, food and consumer goods become more expensive.

Agriculture, Fishing, and Forestry

Most of Myanmar's people work in farming or a farming-related business. The central plains of Myanmar hold most of the country's level, fertile land. Farming has thrived in this region for centuries. Agriculture, fishing, and forestry make up about 55 percent of Myanmar's GDP. These activities employ about 60 percent of the country's workers.

Myanmar produces corn, peanuts, beans, sugarcane, cotton, fruit, and the herb lemongrass. Farmers also grow jute, a tough fiber used to make rope. The key food product in Myanmar is rice, grown throughout the central plains and delta regions. Rice cultivation is hard work. Farmers must plant the seedlings by hand. The young crop grows best in watery paddies. The crop requires a steady water supply from irrigation or reliable rainfall. Myanmar was once an important rice exporter. A sharp drop in production forced the country to import this staple food.

The British introduced opium growing in Burma when the country was a colony. Certain ethnic minorities still rely on opium for their livelihood. They grow opium poppies in mountainous northern and eastern Myanmar. They extract a thick sap and then refine this liquid into heroin. Small ethnic armies control opium growing in areas where government control is weak.

NEW MONEY

In 1987 the junta decided to make new money in Myanmar. Suddenly, the notes of 25-, 35-, and 75-kyat were worthless. New 15-, 45-, and 90-kyat notes replaced the old notes. Ne Win wanted people to use these denominations. The idea came from his love of numerology, or the magical influence of numbers, and his favorite number, 9.

Myanmar farmers raise cattle in drier regions, where good pasture is available. Water buffalo pull plows and help in the hard work of drilling for water. These sturdy animals also help to move earth and construction material. Other livestock include pigs, goats, and chickens.

Fish, a vital part of the Burmese diet, are caught offshore. Large schools of shrimp and shellfish live in Myanmar's coastal waters. Farmers also raise fish in ponds built in the plains and delta.

Forests cover about half of Myanmar's land. The country

The fishers of **Inle Lake** are known for their unique style of rowing. They use one arm and one leg to move their light boats across the surface.

boasts the largest rain forests in Southeast Asia. Myanmar also has the world's largest teak forests. This valuable resource provides more than 10 percent of all export earnings. But illegal teak harvesting has become a major problem in eastern Myanmar. In many areas, the government bans the logging and sale of teak. But the government cannot guard all of Myanmar's remote forests. Illegally cut teak logs find a ready market in neighboring Thailand.

◉ Services and Tourism

The service sector provides services to individuals and businesses rather than producing goods. Service industries include banking, health care, tourism, and real estate. The service sector has grown rapidly since the late twentieth century. Together, these businesses make up 32 percent of the GDP and employ about one-third of all workers. Tourism alone accounts for 20 percent of Myanmar's labor force.

Once closed to outside visitors, Myanmar began to encourage tourism in the 1990s. It invested in hotel and airline companies. Laborers repaired historic and sacred sites. New museums opened. Visits to Myanmar also increased after a terrorist bombing on the Indonesian island of Bali in 2002. Many travelers to Southeast Asia chose Myanmar as a safer place to travel.

Visitors come to see the country's wealth of Buddhist temples. In many regions, unspoiled forests and mountain valleys offer hiking, rafting, and climbing. Along the coast, a few areas have become beach destinations. Small seaside resorts offer scuba diving, snorkeling, surfing, fishing, and other activities.

Transportation and Communications

Myanmar Railways links large towns and the major cities. The system includes about 2,485 miles (4,000 km) of railroads. Few Burmese own cars. For that reason, passenger buses are the most popular way to

Passengers board a crowded bus in Yangon. Buses are a popular means of transport, in part because government policies keep the price of gas high.

travel. Bus travel, however, can be slow. Most of the 16,777 miles (27,000 km) of roads remain unpaved.

Myanmar has eighty-four airports. Most offer only unpaved landing strips for light aircraft. The Yangon International Airport is the country's main air hub. Myanma Airways operates flights within Myanmar and to other countries in the region.

In Myanmar the government limits access to books, journals, and electronic media. The state controls all publishing and broadcasting in the country. The junta uses television and radio to support its decisions and policies. The government also closely monitors use of the Internet. Computers and dial-up service are costly. Most people must use Internet cafés. They can only access websites created in Myanmar. The government reads personal and business e-mail. Anyone criticizing the military junta risks arrest and time in prison.

The *New Light of Myanmar* is an English-language daily newspaper. It prints stories from foreign reporters and media. But all newspaper editors answer to government authorities. Those who print negative stories are subject to arrest and the loss of their jobs. Many Myanmar writers have seen their careers cut short for expressing their opinions.

About 80 percent of the country has access to television broadcasting. Many people gather in restaurants or tea shops to watch. Myanmar Television broadcasts in the evening. This network carries news broadcasts, sports, music, and some foreign cable reports, such as Cable News Network (CNN). Within Myanmar the government-run Radio Myanmar broadcasts throughout the country. Radio stations carry programs in the main minority languages, including Mon and Shan. Broadcasts from outside the country are available to any receiver. The British Broadcasting Corporation (BBC), Voice of America, and Radio Free Asia offer news, opinion, and entertainment

TO VISIT OR NOT TO VISIT?

Tourism in Myanmar remains a thorny political issue. Many opponents of the military regime believe the junta uses tourism to support its tyranny. Aung San Suu Kyi, for example, discourages tourists from visiting. She claims that the ordinary people of Myanmar do not benefit from tourism income. Others believe that outside visitors can encourage the government to open itself to democracy, free elections, and a multiparty system. In addition, in a nation with a tightly controlled media, tourists serve as witnesses to problems and conflicts in Myanmar for the outside world.

free of government censorship. But those listening to these stations risk arrest.

Energy, Mining, and Manufacturing

The industry sector in Myanmar supplies 13 percent of the GDP. Mining, manufacturing, and energy employ about 7 percent of the labor force. The most important industrial sector is oil. Myanmar has the largest oil deposits in Southeast Asia. It has been drilling and selling its oil since 1889.

The government-controlled oil business in Myanmar provides most of the country's foreign trade earnings. All the oil fields lie in the central plains and valley of the Ayeyarwady River. But to reach new deposits, the country must improve and repair drilling equipment. Production has been falling, but new oil exploration is taking place in offshore fields.

LIVELY ISLANDS

In the Mergui Archipelago, business is good. The hundreds of large and small islands offer shelter from the police. This makes smuggling lucrative. Many consumer goods and illegal drugs travel between Thailand and Myanmar through the islands. In addition, local workers harvest pearls and sea cucumbers (edible sea animals). They also collect a special kind of bird's nest. This nest is popular in China and Japan as an ingredient in soup. Visitors here must take care. Smugglers carry guns, and many pirates also sail these waters. They sometimes attack boats and rob the passengers.

Myanmar also extracts natural gas. Gas from the large Yadana and Yetagun gas fields is shipped to Thailand. Myanmar is also developing new gas fields offshore. Korea and India have joined this venture.

Important minerals include copper, tin, iron ore, coal, lead, silver, and gold. Myanmar also mines tungsten. This mineral has a high melting point and goes into light-bulb filaments. Gemstones are an important export and source of foreign earnings. Myanmar supplies most of the world's rubies. It is also an important source of jade and sapphires. Small mining companies ship the uncut gems around the world for processing.

Little investment has been made in manufacturing in Myanmar. Oil refining has been a vital industry for more than a century. Wood mills process timber into sawn wood. Smaller factories make cement, steel, cigarettes, processed food, and refined sugar.

Ruby mines employ most of the inhabitants of the **Mogok valley.** Mining equipment ranges from simple shovels to expensive, high-tech machinery.

Myanmar was once an important clothing producer. Its principal trading partner in this business, however, was the United States. When that nation cut off trade with Myanmar in 1997, clothing and textile industries suffered.

Myanmar's energy comes from oil, thermal energy (which taps underground heat), and hydropower from running water. Dams and turbines generate electricity from running water. The government is planning large hydropower projects on the Thanlwin River. The four dams of this project will generate electricity for use in the country. The rest will go to neighboring Thailand. But Karen and Shan groups protest the damage and disruption that will be caused by dam construction.

◐ Foreign Trade and the Black Market

With the help of oil income, Myanmar has achieved a surplus in foreign trade. The country also exports natural gas as well as teak, clothing, fish, metals, gemstones, and rubber. Its main customers are Thailand, India, China, and Japan. Myanmar imports machinery, transportation equipment, and food. One-third of the country's

The ripe pods of these **opium poppies** are ready to be harvested and processed to produce heroin. Most of Myanmar's illegal opium farms are located in Shan State.

imports come from China. Other key sources of goods are Singapore, Thailand, South Korea, and Malaysia.

Myanmar carries out a busy trade with China along the border, particularly at the town of Mu-Se. From the Myanmar side, trucks deliver vegetables, fruit, and rattan. They return with electronic and consumer goods.

By some estimates, the black market, or illegal trade, in imports and exports makes up about half of the total foreign trade in Myanmar. Smugglers deal in illegal and restricted goods such as cigarettes, teak, and electronic goods. The black market is especially active in Myanmar's remote border regions.

Myanmar also is a major producer of raw opium. Farmers illegally grow opium poppies. At the proper season, they collect dried resin from the seedpods of the poppy. They send the resin to small factories. Workers refine the sap into the illegal drug heroin, then ship it across the country's borders to smugglers in China and Thailand. Myanmar is the world's second-largest producer of illegal opium, after Afghanistan.

The Future

Myanmar's troubled modern history and weak economy have left the country one of the poorest and most isolated in the world. The regime will not allow free elections or free speech. The country's leaders keep the most popular political figure in the country, Aung San Suu Kyi, under house arrest. They censor the media and allow no criticism or questioning of government policy. This prevents open discussion on the best way to meet Myanmar's challenges.

In an attempt to improve the economy, Myanmar has opened up to foreign investment. The country is also investing in tourism. Foreign companies, especially rapidly growing manufacturing businesses from China, see Myanmar as a source of inexpensive labor. But the benefits of this investment don't reach ordinary workers. Many toil under poor working conditions and earn low wages.

The country is also struggling with serious social problems. The government spends most of its budget on its powerful military instead of on education or health care. Many people in the countryside face health problems and malnutrition from poor diets. AIDS has struck harder in Myanmar than elsewhere in Southeast Asia. Unemployment is high. Yet the government prevents people from emigrating. Such conditions lead to rising frustration. Without change, this frustration could lead to violence. For this reason, Myanmar has many tough challenges ahead and faces an uncertain future.

Timeline

CA. 3000 B.C.   Earliest known inhabitants live in Myanmar.

302 B.C.   The Mon people from central Asia establish their first kingdom.

CA. A.D. 100   The Pyu from Tibet have established several city-states in Myanmar.

800s   The Bamars build a capital city at Bagan. Chinese armies overrun the Pyu states.

1057   King Anawrahta defeats the Mon and unifies Burma.

1287   The Mongols defeat the Burmese at the Battle of Vochan.

1435   The Venetian Nicoto di Conti, the first European to visit Burma, arrives in Bagan.

1541   Burmese battle Europeans over trading privileges at Martaban.

1613   King Anaukpetlun defeats Philip de Brito of Portugal and reunites the Bamar kingdom.

1752   The Mon capture Inwa, the new Bamar capital.

1819   The British invade Burma for the first time.

1852   The British invade Lower Burma and capture Bagan and Rangoon (modern Yangon).

1857   Mindon Min builds a new palace and capital at Mandalay.

1885   The Third Anglo-Burmese War breaks out. Britain makes Burma a part of its colony of India.

1920   The University of Rangoon opens in Rangoon, the capital of the British colony.

1923   A Burmese legislature meets for the first time. It has limited power to make law or policy in the colony.

1930   Saya San leads a revolt in the countryside.

1937   Britain makes Burma a colony separate from India.

1942   Japan invades and occupies Burma, sweeping away the British colonial government.

1945   Burmese and Allied forces drive the Japanese out of Burma.

1948   Burma wins independence from British rule.

1962   General Ne Win leads a military coup against the government and seizes power.

1988 The government puts down demonstrations against military rule. Police and army troops kill hundreds of people.

1990 The National League for Democracy (NLD) wins national elections by a large majority. The government does not allow the winning candidates to take their seats in the legislature, however, and instead jails and exiles opposition leaders.

1992 General Than Shwe replaces Saw Maung as head of the State Law and Order Restoration Council (SLORC).

1997 The SLORC renames itself the State Peace and Development Council.

2003 In protest of the house arrest of Aung San Suu Kyi, the United States bans all trade with Myanmar.

2006 The junta extends Aung San Suu Kyi's house arrest for another year.

2007 The government unveils the new capital city of Naypyidaw and allows a few members of the foreign media to report directly from Myanmar for the first time.

COUNTRY NAME Union of Myanmar

AREA 261,789 square miles (678,034 sq. km)

MAIN LANDFORMS Ayeyarwady Delta region, Central Plateau, Rakhine range, Hengduan Shan range, Shan Plateau, Tanintharyi region, Bilauktaung Mountains

HIGHEST POINT Mount Hkakabo, 19,295 feet (5,881 m) above sea level

MAJOR RIVERS Ayeyarwady, Thanlwin, Chindwin

ANIMALS Banteng, bears, cobras, elephants, fruit bats, kraits, leopards, parrots, peacocks, rhinoceroses, sea turtles, snakes, tapirs, tigers, thrushes, vipers, wild pigs

CAPITAL CITY Yangon, gradually moving to Naypyidaw (formerly Pyinmana)

OTHER MAJOR CITIES Mandalay, Mawlamyine, Pathein

OFFICIAL LANGUAGE Burmese

MONETARY UNIT kyat. 1 kyat = 100 pyas.

MYANMAR CURRENCY

The kyat has been the currency of Myanmar since 1952. In 1987 the government completely changed the kyat to notes of 15, 45, and 90 kyats. This change caused great unrest among the population, as old kyat notes suddenly became worthless. In 1989 the government then introduced the current system of notes, with 1, 5, 10, 20, 45, 50, 90, 100, 200, 500, and 1,000-kyat notes. The largest denomination shows an engraving of the Central Bank of Myanmar. Other notes show mythological figures, important Burmese of the past, and scenes of people at work. The kyat is divided into 100 pyas. There are 100-pya and 50-pya notes, as well as pya coins, but they are rarely seen and almost worthless. The official exchange rate of the kyat is about 6 to the U.S. dollar. However, a black market in the currency sells between 1,000 and 1,200 kyats for 1 dollar.

Currency Fast Facts

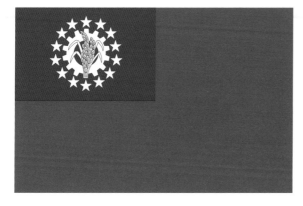

The flag of Myanmar is red with a blue rectangle in the upper left side. Fourteen white stars circle a central field, which depicts a cogwheel and a stalk of rice. These symbols represent the union of industry and agriculture and of factory workers and farmers. The fourteen stars represent the seven divisions and seven states of Myanmar. The red of the flag represents courage, and the blue symbolizes integrity, peace, and endurance. The white of the stars stands for purity and honor. Myanmar adopted the flag on January 3, 1974, when the country officially became the Socialist Republic of the Burmese Federation. Although the official name of the country has changed, the flag remains the same.

The first national song of Burma was "Dobama Asiayone," or "We Bamars." The song served as a rallying cry for Bamars fighting against Japanese occupation during World War II. In 1947 the government selected a new anthem. The composer Saya Tin wrote "Kam Ba Ma Kyei" ("Till the End of the World, Myanmar"). He was also the author of "We Bamars." In 1950 the government awarded him a title of honor, Wunna Kyaw Htin (The Beautiful and Famous), for his song.

"Kam Ba Ma Kyei"

Till the end of the world, Myanmar!
Since she is the true inheritance from our forefathers,
we love and value her.
We will fight and give our lives for the union.
This is the country and land of our own.
For her prosperity, we will responsibly shoulder the task,
Standing as one in duty to our precious land.

Note: Most people in Myanmar do not have last names. Each multi-part name is a whole name. (Aung San Suu Kyi is an exception. Her father's name is part of her name to honor his importance.) "U" is a title of respect, similar to "Mr." "Daw" is the title for women.

ANAWRAHTA (?–1077) A famous king of the Bamars, Anawrahta began his reign in 1044. He conquered the Mon people and captured their capital of Thaton in 1057, bringing thirty thousand prisoners back to his own capital of Bagan. This event united Burma for the first time. Anawrahta also converted Burma to Theravada Buddhism, the faith that dominates modern Myanmar. He also initiated two centuries of temple building in Bagan that left the city with thousands of pagodas.

AUNG SAN (1915–1947) Aung San was a military and revolutionary leader born in Natmauk. After attending the University of Rangoon, he joined the anticolonial movement. He was head of an organization known as We Bamars. He joined the Japanese during World War II to fight the British, but later he led the fight to drive the Japanese from the country. He served under the British until signing an independence agreement with the British in January 1947. On July 19, 1947, a group of six men loyal to a rival politician assassinated him and six other cabinet members. The day of this event is celebrated every year in Myanmar as Martyrs' Day.

AUNG SAN SUU KYI (b. 1945) A leader of the pro-democracy movement, Aung San Suu Kyi is the daughter of Aung San. She was born in Yangon and attended college in England. In 1988 Suu Kyi became an outspoken critic of the Myanmar regime. Although her party won the 1990 elections, the junta did not permit her to take power. Instead, the junta placed her under house arrest. She remains confined to her family's house in Yangon. She is the author of *Freedom from Fear* and other books. She won the Nobel Peace Prize in 1991.

BA MAW (1893–1977) A political leader born in Maubin, Ba Maw went to college in France. He first made his name in Burma as a lawyer. He defended the leader Saya San after Saya San's rebellion of 1930 against British rule. Ba Maw served as premier of the colony from 1937 to 1939. He became Burma's head of state while the country was under Japanese occupation in 1943. In the 1960s, the government of General Ne Win arrested and imprisoned him without charge. While in prison, he wrote a manuscript that later became *Breakthrough in Burma: Memoirs of a Revolution 1939–1946*.

JAMES HLA KYAW (1886–1920) A writer born in Shwegyin, James Hla Kyaw worked as a translator for the colony's government. Poor health convinced him to resign his job and take up writing. He was inspired by the French author Alexandre Dumas's novel *The Count of Monte Cristo* to write *Maung Yin Maung Ma Me Ma*. (The title is two lovers' names.) This was the first modern novel written in Burmese. Before this work, Burmese literature did not have a tradition of long novels.

LUDU DAW AMAR (b. 1915) A leading writer and outspoken critic of the Myanmar regime, Ludu Daw Amar first gained fame in the 1930s with her translation of *Trial in Burma*, a book by Maurice Collis. With her husband, she started the journal *Ludu*, or "The People," after World War II. In 1949 the Burmese army destroyed the magazine's offices. The army believed her to be a Communist. She also wrote a book titled *Amay Shay Sagaa*, or "Mother's Old Sayings." This work attacks modern music and customs that the author believes degrade traditional Burmese culture.

MAR MAR AYE (b. 1940) This singer, actress, and author was born in Myon Mya. While still a teenager, she became one of the best-known vocalists in Burma. During the 1960s and 1970s, she worked as a radio producer. She has written articles and novels and acted in three movies, one of which, *The Sound of Emerald Bells*, was nominated for an Academy Award. She lives in the United States.

THAN SHWE (b. 1933) The head of state of Myanmar since 1992, General Than Shwe was born in Kyaukse. He joined the army at the age of twenty. After the coup of 1988, the junta appointed him to the State Law and Order Restoration Council (SLORC). He changed the country's name to Myanmar in 1989. In 1992 he replaced General Saw Maung as chairman of the SLORC. He made closer ties with neighboring countries and made it easier for tourists to visit Myanmar. However, he has kept many opponents under arrest, including Aung San Suu Kyi. A rule forces members of the SLORC to retire at the age of sixty. However, Than Shwe has made an exception for himself.

U THANT (1909–1974) U Thant was an educator and international diplomat born in Pantanaw. He represented Burma in the United Nations (UN) beginning in 1953. In 1961 he published a three-volume *History of Postwar Burma*. In the same year, he became the leader of the UN as its secretary-general. While at the helm of the UN, he dealt with many international crises, including the Vietnam War (1957–1975). He died in 1974. His funeral in Burma grew into a nationwide demonstration against the military regime that ruled the country.

THAN TUN (1923–2005) Born in the village of Daunggyi in the delta region, Than Tun was Myanmar's best-known historian. He taught at Mandalay University. He wrote the *Royal Orders of Burma*, a ten-volume history of the country, and many other history books. But the military government did not allow them to be published or sold inside Myanmar. Than Tun angered Myanmar's leaders by not agreeing with their view of the country's history.

BAGAN The historic capital city of the Burmese kingdom is also known as the City of Four Million Pagodas. It lies on the east bank of the Ayeyarwady River. Many old temples dot the surrounding countryside. The most famous is the tenth-century Shwezigon Pagoda. This temple houses several relics of the Buddha, including a bone and a tooth.

THE GOLDEN ROCK, MOUNT KYAIKTIYO The Golden Rock is a small stupa (shrine) perched on a rock. It balances high on a cliffside on Mount Kyaiktiyo, in Mon State. Gold leaf covers the rock and makes it shine in the daylight. According to the legend of the Golden Rock, the boulder balances by a hair of the Buddha's head. A wandering monk placed the hair under the rock in the tenth century.

HPO WIN DAUNG CAVES Near the town of Monywa and the Chindwin River are a series of hillside caves. Over centuries, artists carved more than 400,000 images of the Buddha into the sandstone. Painted murals also adorn the caves. Some are more than five hundred years old. A small pack of trained monkeys guides visitors through the caves.

INLE LAKE This picturesque lake lies 2,953 feet (900 m) above sea level in the Shan State. Floating islands of vegetation drift around the lake. There are also markets and small villages built on stilts in the lake. The famous fishers of Inle Lake paddle with one leg, freeing their hands to catch fish with nets.

MOUNT POPA This peak reaches 4,987 feet (1,520 m) in central Myanmar. On its summit is the Mahagiri Shrine. The Burmese believe this shrine houses spirits that live on the mountaintop. Mount Popa is also home to a sandalwood plantation. This aromatic shrub provides the base for a popular kind of incense.

ROYAL PALACE, MANDALAY This is a reconstruction of the king's palace in Mandalay. Intense fighting between the British and Japanese destroyed most of the original building in 1945. Only the walls, towers, and moat survived. The new version includes reconstructions of watchtowers and the audience hall, where the king received visitors. It also includes the original tomb of King Mindon Min, who built the first palace in 1857.

SHWEDAGON PAGODA, YANGON The Shwedagon Pagoda is a famous Buddhist shrine in Yangon. Its huge half-dome ends in a tall spire painted in gold leaf. The spire reaches 326 feet (99 m) high. The shrine was begun in the sixth century B.C., when two traders of the Mon kingdom returned from India with several hairs from the Buddha's head. Queen Shin Sawbu completed the shrine in the fifteenth century. Skilled workers added a marble terrace, Buddha statues, many large bells, smaller prayer halls, and gem-studded ornaments.

Anglo-Burmese Wars: three conflicts between the British and Burmese between 1824 and 1885 that ended with Burma becoming a British colony

animism: a system of belief in the spirits of nature, which have influence over one's life and fortunes

colony: an area or people under the control of a foreign power

deforestation: the loss of forests due to logging or clearing land for human uses. Deforestation leads to soil erosion, loss of wildlife habitat, and global warming (the gradual rise in Earth's temperature).

ethnic minorities: those groups in Myanmar not belonging to the dominant Bamar culture. The largest groups of ethnic minorities are the Shan, Kachin, Karen, Mon, Chin, and Rakhine.

gross domestic product (GDP): the total value of the country's goods and services produced in one year

guerrillas: small groups of rebel fighters who operate independently and engage in nontraditional warfare, such as hit-and-run strikes

junta: a ruling group or committee of military leaders. A junta runs Myanmar and allows no open opposition to its rule.

literacy: the ability to read and write a basic sentence

longyi: a traditional garment reaching from the waist to the calves, worn by men, women, and children in Myanmar

monsoon: a seasonal rain and wind that blows from the seas over Myanmar and throughout Southeast Asia

nats: spirits that originate in the animist beliefs of ancient Burma. Myanmar's thirty-seven official nats exist alongside Buddhist beliefs and are closely connected to daily life.

Pali: a scholarly language used for the sacred texts and chants of Buddhism

peninsula: a fingerlike portion of land jutting out into water, connected on one side to a larger piece of land

rain forest: a woodland that grows in areas with high annual rainfall. Rain forest treetops form a continuous canopy (roof), so the forest floor does not receive much sunlight.

tea shop: a popular public gathering place in Myanmar, where friends meet to drink tea and talk

Thakin: "masters," a group of people, many of them university students and professors, who gathered in the 1920s to oppose British rule of Burma

thanaka paste: a substance made from thanaka bark, which women and children in Myanmar apply to their faces to protect themselves from the sun and as decoration

Theravada Buddhism: the belief system that dominates religious life and thought in Myanmar. The other major Buddhist system, Mahayana, is followed by Chinese and other immigrants.

Glossary

Selected Bibliography

Abbott, Gerry. *The Traveller's History of Burma*. Bangkok, Thailand: Orchid Press, 2000.
A collection of descriptions of Myanmar by those who visited the country in earlier times.

"Burma." *CIA World Factbook*. November 2, 2006.
https://www.cia.gov/cia/publications/factbook/geos/bm.html (November 11, 2006).
A site giving detailed background information on Myanmar (still officially Burma to the U.S. government) and its geography, history, economy, and political issues.

Callahan, Mary. *Making Enemies: War and State Building in Burma*. Ithaca, NY: Cornell University Press, 2003.
The author describes how the Burmese military became the most powerful institution in the country after World War II and how this led to the military takeover of the country in 1962.

Clark, Michael, and Joe Cummings. *Myanmar (Burma)*. Hawthorn, AU: Lonely Planet Publications, 2002.
This guidebook covers Myanmar's geography, climate, and conditions and contains a good introduction to Burmese history and culture.

Falconer, John. *Burmese Design and Architecture*. Hong Kong: Periplus Editions, 2001.
A history of Burmese design, from ancient to modern, in art and architecture.

The Far East and Australasia 2006. London: Routledge, 2005.
Part of the Europa Regional Surveys of the World, this volume includes a long article on Myanmar.

Klein, William, ed. *Burma/Myanmar*. London: APA Publications, 1996.
This book offers background on Myanmar's history, culture, religion, architecture, and political conditions for visitors to the country.

Marshall, Andrew. *The Trouser People: A Story of Burma in the Shadow of the Empire*. New York: Counterpoint Press, 2003.
The author recounts his travels to many remote and little-known regions of Burma, giving some history and context for the country's political events.

Population Reference Bureau. 2006.
http://www.prb.org (June 2006).
PRB's annual statistics provide in-depth demographics on Myanmar's population, including birth and death rates, infant mortality rates, and other statistics relating to health, environment, education, employment, family planning, and more.

Sardesai, D. R. *Southeast Asia: Past and Present*. Boulder, CO: Westview Press, 1997.
The author gives the economic, political, and military history of the Southeast Asia region, which includes Myanmar, and describes how the countries of this region are linked by religion, culture, and history.

South, Ashley. *Mon Nationalism and Civil War in Burma: The Golden Sheldrake.* **London: Routledge, 2002.**
An account of the Mon, an important ethnic group within Myanmar who controlled a strong and independent state in Lower Burma for many centuries.

Steinberg, David. *Burma: The State of Myanmar.* **Washington, DC: Georgetown University Press, 2002.**
A Myanmar expert analyzes the country's politics, economy, and culture, and how four decades of military rule shaped the modern nation.

Thant Myint-U. *The Making of Modern Burma.* **Cambridge: Cambridge University Press, 2001.**
An academic book about the nineteenth-century Burmese dynasty and its wars with the British Empire.

U.S. Department of State, Bureau of East Asian and Pacific Affairs. *Background Note: Burma.* **2006.**
http://www.state.gov/r/pa/ei/bgn/35910.htm (June 2006).
The background notes of the State Department supply information about the United States' relations with Burma as well as a brief profile of the country's people, history, government, political conditions, economy, and more. The website also provides timely access to official travel and foreign policy information at http://www.state.gov.

Webster, Donovan. *The Burma Road: The Epic Story of the China-Burma-India Theater in World War II.* **New York: Farrar, Straus & Giroux, 2003.**
A history of the Burma campaign during World War II, when the United States and Britain fought Japanese occupation of the country and built a vital road across northern Burma at great cost.

Aung San Suu Kyi. *Aung San of Burma: A Biographical Portrait by His Daughter*. Edinburgh, UK: Kiscadale Publications, 1995.
An account of Burma's nationalist hero, Aung San, written by his daughter. She did research on his life and collected memories from friends and family.

————. *Letters from Burma*. New York: Penguin, 1998.
The democracy leader wrote these fifty-two essays for a Japanese newspaper. They explain the political situation in Burma and also cover Burmese history and culture. She has written two other books about Myanmar, titled *Freedom from Fear* and *Voice of Hope*.

Burma Daily.
http://www.burmadaily.com/
This site provides news articles and travel information, as well as information sources from India and other nations in Southeast Asia.

BurmaNet News.
http://www.burmanet.org/news/
The articles on this website come from Burmese and outside sources. They give current events and news articles concerning Myanmar.

Fink, Christina. *Living Silence: Burma under Military Rule*. London: Zed Books, 2001.
The author describes the effect of military rule on ordinary people.

Khoo Thwe. *From the Land of Green Ghosts: A Burmese Odyssey*. New York: Harper Perennial, 2003.
The author, a student leader, fled Myanmar after the 1988 prodemocracy revolt. He describes his boyhood in a remote village, his fight against the military junta, and his life as a university student in Cambridge, England.

Larkin, Emma. *Finding George Orwell in Burma*. New York: The Penguin Press, 2005.
A traveler explores modern Burma, searching for the traces of George Orwell. This British writer set his first novel, *Burmese Days*, in the country, drawing on his own experience.

Lintner, Bertil. *Outrage: Burma's Struggle for Democracy*. London: White Lotus, 1990.
A description of the democracy movement in Burma during the 1980s and the violent crackdown by the military junta in 1988.

Lonely Planet: Myanmar.
http://www.lonelyplanet.com/worldguide/destinations/asia/myanmar/
A visitor's guide to Myanmar, with sections on its religious and cultural life, sights to see, events, festivals, and choices for adventure travel. The site includes a discussion on whether to visit Myanmar and, in doing so, lend support to its military regime.

Mawdsley, James. *The Iron Road: A Stand for Truth and Democracy in Burma*. New York: North Point Press, 2002.
The author travels to Burma to protest the Burmese government's crackdown and the jailing of Aung San Suu Kyi. He describes his arrest, torture, and five-year imprisonment in Burma.

Further Reading and Websites

Myanmar.com
http://www.myanmar.com

The official website of the government of Myanmar has links to official media outlets and sections on the arts, lifestyle topics, current news, and travel tips.

Orwell, George. *Burmese Days*. New York: Harper and Brothers, 1934.

A novel about colonial Burma by the English writer who would later create *Animal Farm* and *1984*. Orwell served in the colonial police in Burma during the 1920s when Burma was under British rule.

Saw Myat Yin. *Myanmar*. Tarrytown, NY: Marshall Cavendish, 2002.

This book is part of the Cultures of the World series for younger readers. Well illustrated with photos and charts, information is presented about Myanmar's geography, history, government, economy, environment, and people.

Smith, Roland, and Michael J. Schmidt. *In the Forest with the Elephants*. New York: Harcourt Brace & Company, 1998.

This book describes the lives of Myanmar's five thousand working elephants, which learn to handle baggage and timber at the command of trainers known as oozies.

Stewart, Whitney. *Aung San Suu Kyi: Fearless Voice of Burma*. Minneapolis: Lerner Publications Company, 1997.

The author traces the life of the prodemocracy leader, from her childhood through her years as a popular spokesperson during the 1988 demonstrations and her house arrest in Yangon.

UN Millenium Development Goals.
http://www.un.org/millenniumgoals/

This site provides all sorts of information about the millennium development goals, which Myanmar agreed to in 2000. The goals range from cutting extreme poverty in half to stopping the spread of HIV/AIDS by 2015.

vgsbooks.com
http://www.vgsbooks.com

Visit vgsbooks.com, the home page of the Visual Geography Series®. You can get linked to all sorts of useful on-line information, including geographical, historical, demographic, cultural, and economic websites. The vgsbooks.com site is a great resource for late-breaking news and statistics.

Wong, Kenneth. *A Prayer for Burma*. Santa Monica, CA: Santa Monica Press, 2003.

A Burmese American born in Rangoon writes about his return home to Myanmar. He describes his surprise at modern changes in Myanmar and his fascination with traditions that have survived the nation's dictatorship.

Captions for photos appearing on cover and chapter openers:

Cover: The royal barge glides into dock on the moat of the Mandalay Royal Palace.

pp. 4–5 The Bamar people founded the city of Bagan in the middle of the ninth century. The city flourished for centuries. It has become the site of more than 3,000 Buddhist temples, ranging from small ruins to large, gold-covered structures.

pp. 8–9 The Ayeyarwady River flows past the outskirts of Mandalay.

pp. 20–21 Small Buddha statues adorn a temple wall in the town of Nyaungshwe on the shores of Inle Lake.

pp. 36–37 Schoolchildren shade themselves with parasols (sun umbrellas) while waiting in line.

pp. 46–47 Two Buddhist monks visit the Shwedagon Pagoda in Yangon.

pp. 56–57 Farmers work in a rice field north of Yangon.

Photo Acknowledgments
The images in this book are used with the permission of: © Jane Sweeney/Art Directors, pp. 4–5; XNR Productions, pp. 6,10 © Tibor Bognar/Art Directors, pp. 8–9, 17, 40, 44, 45, 48–49; © Robin Smith/Art Directors, pp. 12–13, 38; © age fotostock/SuperStock, pp. 14 (left), 51; © Mary Plage/Oxford Scientific/Jupiterimages, p. 14 (right), © Jean-Léo Dugast/Peter Arnold, Inc., p. 15; © Andrew Gasson/Art Directors, p. 16; © Hemis/Alamy, p. 18; © Andrew Geiger, Inc./The Image Bank/Getty Images, pp. 20–21; © SuperStock, Inc./SuperStock, p. 22; © Mary Evans Picture Library/The Image Works, p. 25; © Keystone/Hulton Archive/Getty Images, p. 27; © Ask Images/Art Directors, p. 31; © Topham/The Image Works, p. 33; © Khin Maung Win/AFP/Getty Images, pp. 34, 56–57; © Graham Grieves/Art Directors, pp. 36–37; © Liverani-UNEP/Peter Arnold, Inc., p. 39; © Jon Arnold Images/SuperStock, p. 41; © Shehzad Noorani/Peter Arnold, Inc., p. 43; © Saeed Khan/ AFP/Getty Images, pp. 46–47; © Jean-Léo Dugast/Panos Pictures, pp. 52, 59, 63; © STR/AFP/ Getty Images, p. 60; © Marcus Rose/Insight/Panos Pictures, p. 64; © Michele Burgess/SuperStock, p. 68.

Front Cover: © Tibor Bognar/Art Directors. Back Cover: NASA.